HOW TO SUCCEED WITH WOMEN

by
Anthony F. Badalamenti, PhD

Copyright © 1992, 1995, 2000 by Anthony F. Badalamenti

All rights reserved. No part of this book may be reproduced or transmitted in any form or by any means, electronic or mechanical, including photocopy, recording or any information storage or retrieval system, without prior permission in writing from the author.

Library of Congress Catalog Card Number   00-090596
ISBN   0-9648590-1-7

Published by Scientific Support
Westwood, New Jersey

THIS BOOK WAS WRITTEN TO BRING YOU THE VERY BEST IN LIFE

HOW TO SUCCEED WITH WOMEN

Preface To The New Edition

Many men, and some women, have reported the benefits of reading this book. Most also gave worthwhile suggestions on how to improve it. This new and expanded version replies gratefully to all of them.

There are a number of major upgrades in this version. For one, narratives from singles' coaching of men and women have been added. Such examples quickly bring the material and the important issues to life in the words of people who have worked to master them. Second, the exercises are now guided, meaning that the exercises are done in sample format to jump start you.

The original two parts have been retained in all essentials and comprise Parts I and II, THE BASICS OF SUCCESS and AFTER THE BASICS OF SUCCESS. A third part has been added, SPECIAL SUCCESS ISSUES. This treats such issues as shyness, the intellectual man, and a number of cultural myths that stand in the way of success. A final part, MAKING IT HAPPEN, has also been added. It brings all

2 How to Succeed With Women

the material together to help you take it into your life and create the success you want.

The appendix on Success FAQs is also new. It is based on response to the website Success FAQs on Singles, Dating & Relationships (URL www.success-ways.com). The answers to the FAQs address the most common concerns of men on love and romance.

HOW TO SUCCEED WITH WOMEN
Original Preface To The First Edition

The pages that follow combine insight and method to help you achieve your goals as a male who wants to succeed with women. Success may mean winning the girl of your dreams for a permanent relation. It could mean becoming more proficient at meeting women, or at dating and getting to know them. You may want to better understand what a relation involves psychologically. Whatever your goals are, my objective is to stir in you those feelings and attitudes that will create your success. I also give you a great deal of practical information to help you, especially in making a first connection. Insight helps, so does action. You need both and I try to bring you to both. Nothing is more effective in life than informed action.

Two streams meet to create this book. Twenty years of work in psychiatric research contribute deep insights into the makeup of women. Fifteen years of involvement with the single lifestyle industry provides intimate knowledge of the practical problems facing the single male. The fusion of these approaches, one grounded in theory and the other in practice, results in a reliable guide for the single male who wishes to take action and to be confident of his outcome.

The material in this book has worked remarkably well for me. It has worked so well that many men have asked me to write a book about how to do it. I took up their suggestion remembering how I once wished for more from the world of the single male. If you live in that world and want to draw its rewards then this book is for you. Its spirit and its practical advice will help you to succeed.

Getting the Most from This Book

It is as impossible for a man to be cheated by anyone but himself, as for a thing to be, and not to be, at the same time.

...from Compensation by Ralph Waldo Emerson

If you want to do better with women then this book can change your life. It will tell you what women are like on the inside and what they really want. You will enter their world and learn how they see you. You will no longer see them as strange, difficult or inscrutable. The experience will transform your life as you work with it. It will put you in touch with the male forces in you that women spend their entire lives searching for. You will learn that you have a magical hold over women just as strong as the one they have over you.

Every chapter but the last two ends by giving you exercises in the material. Do them. To read this book and not do the exercises is to miss much of its benefit. The exercises will help you to more fully understand the material and how it works. More importantly, they will help you to live the material and create the success you want. Spend time with them and watch your rewards come in faster and faster.

Many of the exercises rely on the highly effective technique of visualization. It is an enjoyable method that comes naturally to most people and is quickly mastered. You can greatly increase the rate at which your success grows by following the instructions and working to build your skill at it. Adding visualization helps you to advance from reading the material to living it and putting it to work for you.

Your first reading of this book will increase your success and your understanding of women. I recommend reading it again from time to time because the meaning and use of the material grows from one stage of your life to the next. Each next reading will bring more skill and wisdom to your love life because each next stage of life increases your powers.

Before you get underway I want to share with you an experience I had while writing this book. I was at a party talking to a very attractive woman whose demeanor made me feel that she had a great deal to offer. Our conversation drifted to my work on this book. She asked for some examples of the techniques that I felt work so well. I told her about a procedure that I later name the umbrella technique in this book. Her mouth and eyes opened wide as she said with a gesture of happy helplessness, "My goodness! Why don't you just go and tell all our secrets"? Bon appetit!

TABLE OF CONTENTS

PART I: THE BASICS OF SUCCESS

1. What Is Really Different? — page 11
2. An Important Difference — page 21
3. How Women See Men — page 31
4. What Do Women Want in Relationships? — page 41
5. Flirting: The First Encounter — page 49
6. Finesse in Flirting: The Umbrella Technique — page 61
7. Getting to Know Her — page 73
8. Endings and Beginnings — page 81
9. Starting Fresh — page 93
10. Irresistible Men — page 105
11. The Darker Side of Women — page 121

PART II: AFTER THE BASICS OF SUCCESS

12. The Lure of the Knight — page 133
13. Dates, Mates and More — page 143
14. The Immortal Male — page 155
15. Around and Through Female Ambivalence — page 165
16. Wily Women — page 175
17. Playfulness Never Fails — page 185
18. Casting Sexual Spells — page 197

PART III: SPECIAL SUCCESS ISSUES

19. Shyness — page 213
20. The Intellectual — page 223

21. Myths: Lines and Ploys page 233
22. Older Men, Younger Women page 245
23. More Myths: The Handsome Man,
　　Wealth and Power page 255

PART IV: MAKING IT HAPPEN

24. The Art of Success page 271
25. Position Yourself for Success page 287

APPENDIX: SUCCESS FAQs page 297

PART I
THE BASICS OF SUCCESS

Part I gives you the basic elements of success. Its opening chapter alerts you to the surprising lack of difference between the genders. This perspective creates some immediate confidence with the knowledge that males and females are far more alike than different. It also opens the way to easier communication from male to female. The differences that are really there are presented next. A view from the other side, on how women see men and what they expect versus hope for from men, then follows.

The material builds mostly to the crucial moment of first encounter, to what women wish to find at that time and how to manage it. How to flirt, grow a relationship, learn from it and what to be on the look out for are also presented.

Chapter 1.

What Is Really Different?

And here's the happy bounding flea—
You cannot tell the he from she.
The sexes look alike, you see;
But she can tell, and so can he.

...from the Flea by Roland Young

Just before starting to work on the present version of this book, I had an interesting experience with a client, call him Bob. He began with issues of low self esteem and some anxiety. Within about a year he felt good enough about himself to demand more from life. He felt he was doing well enough at work but wanted to make progress with women who struck him as a complete mystery. When I encouraged Bob to get his feet wet and to return with news of how he did, our relation evolved into success coaching.

Our exchange in the early part of his efforts to connect, given below, shows what little awareness most men have of the opening issue in learning how to succeed with women. The initials AFB are mine.

Bob: I went and tried my luck at a few singles' events.

AFB: How did it go?
Bob: There were some really attractive women. I had no idea how to connect with them. I felt like a visitor to another country with a different language and customs.
AFB: What made it feel strange?
Bob: I understood where the men were coming from because I was in the same place. I envied how well some of them did. But the women, what did they want? What were they about? What is the first step? Obviously, flirting is the first step but how do you do that and make it work?
AFB: It sounds like the feeling of strangeness is coming from a wish to understand them versus you. Is that it?
Bob: That's sounds right. At first I see how seductive and desirable they are. That makes me want to connect with them. Then I think to myself, how can I do that and I become anxious because I have no answer. I get stuck because I don't understand them and I have no idea of what they want.
AFB: You make it sound like they are worlds apart from you.
Bob: That's just how it feels. They're beautiful, I want them, but I have no idea where they are coming from or what they want.
AFB: It pays to see that they are much more like you than different from you.
Bob: You're putting me on, aren't you?
AFB: No, really.

Bob then asked me to elaborate on my position that men and women are much more alike than different. We had a lively exchange about the great absence of

What Is Really Different? 13

differences between the genders. This news usually hits a man like a thunderbolt with feelings of disbelief and hope at the same time. The first because it doesn't sound true, and the second because if it is true, then men are one up on women from the very beginning.

The fact is, most men exaggerate the differences between the sexes, counting too many things in and too few out. A man's physical and psychological experience of himself has much more in common with a woman's than otherwise. In almost every way men and women are more alike than different. When the differences are real, they leap out in sharp contrast against all else that is the same or similar in the male. The first lesson on success with women depends on seeing this, and seeing it makes success become easier.

There are immediate gains in just seeing what differences are real. This understanding spares you the effort of treating everything about a woman as different. This puts you in touch with the real differences that need your attention. It also begins to awaken new and better responses to them, simply because you begin to look in the right places and stop wasting time looking for differences where there are none.

This insight alone will make things easier in a few ways. For one, you will become aware of all you already have in common with women and see that there is a large basis for a first exchange with them. Making a first connection with them will then seem more familiar and natural because you will not have anxious eyes looking for differences that simply are not there. Your attention will go at first to what your nature and hers have in common and then move on to studying what is really different.

Science verifies that men and women are much more alike than different. When I told Bob that the genetic make up of a human, male or female, and a chimpanzee are about 98% the same, I thought he would fall through the floor. The physiologies of men and women are almost identical. This is why, with the exception of the reproductive system and the emotional centers of the brain, medical texts present the same material for both sexes. Every feature that is prominent in one gender corresponds to a lesser feature in the other. This is easy to see with breasts versus pectoral muscles, a man's penis and testicles versus a woman's clitoris and labia, or rounded female versus flat male buttocks. When a physician diagnoses a patient, most of the inferences are made in the same way for both genders. Most of the time, the things we see as different are made so by our culture and not by our biology.

The experience of the inner self is similar for both sexes. A woman's hopes for her friends, family and community are very much like a man's. Her experience of the desire for satisfying work is essentially the same as a man's. She will show happiness for a job well done and anxiety over uncertainty the same way a man does. The fact is, each sex has all the inner workings of the other with most of the differences found in how much one gender has a given strength when compared to the other.

Women are more aware of these things than men are. History has made it so. Until recently, it was a given that a woman would become a mother and attend to all the important moment to moment needs of children. Countless ages of nursing both sexes have sensitized them to doing this very well. There is more on this real gender difference in the next paragraph, but for now put yourself in the position of the mothering person and ask how different does a female infant look from a male? Even a physician has take to a studied look at a newborn to see if it is male or female. The obvious physical differences appear later and they are more subtle than most people assume. For example, it is a popular sport in many places for a male to dress like a female, easily fooling people and duping them into embarrassing actions, such as a male flirting with male he thinks is a female. This kind of spoofing goes the other way too. Most of the cues to a person being male or female are in how the person dresses and presents, not in how the person is formed.

There are some differences, not many, that are real and history has exaggerated them for reasons that no longer exist. For most of recorded history the closer part of child rearing went to the female without question. Women were taught from early on that their role was in caring for the family, in being its heart and loving support. For countless ages their view of themselves formed around creating and upholding life. The close relationship with the child and its budding personality drew their energy to forming emotional and intuitive powers needed for their role. At that early time the greater strength of the male was sent to deal with the hazards of life found in a hostile world. The male hunted, protected and developed a lore of bravery.

Myths were formed to define roles for male and female and to dignify them. Ideal images of a loving wife and mother of great sensitivity and surpassing beauty, and of an extraordinary male hunter with superhuman powers sprang from them. The myths went to the tribal young as stories instructing them in their gender roles, filling them with energy for their predefined places in life. And so the idea of an immense gender divide became part of the tribal cultures all around the world. The societies that later grew from these tribes only recently began to question the myths that long ago and far away did much to help the race to grow and prosper.

But even in those long ago times, each gender saw at some level that men and women were not all that different. Each gender noticed the ways and messages of the other and silently learned from them. Keeping the silence was a good idea in a world that needed to maintain the fiction of an immense gender difference. We are no longer in that world where each sex has to muffle how much it sees the other in itself. The world is coming to terms with how alike rather than different the genders are. Finding what is shared by both sexes can only charm each into discovering what differences are really there and enjoying them so much more.

You will need to deepen your awareness of just how much alike the sexes are to succeed more with women. You can begin work on this now. Try to find something, anything, in yourself that you feel women do not experience. Read the next sentence before you get lost in trying to make this happen. There is nothing in you or about you that you won't find in a woman. It's all

What Is Really Different?   17

a question of who has it more. What is in you is also in a woman but chances are you have more of it. It goes the other way too. Try to find something from a woman's make up that you think men don't have and test it against your own experience. Again, don't get lost in the process because there is no such thing. It's worth sending you on a wild goose chase to get you to see clearly that each sex has everything of the other but in different proportions. And it is a fact that where the differences count the proportions are very different.

Women, who always seem to know these things in the first place, welcome men who see that it is so. When a woman sees that you see what she sees, she then feels connected to you and admires you. Women respond richly to a man who respects them as persons, not too different from himself, with a polite emphasis on the real and obvious sexual differences they prize so highly. Look for this in the next woman you meet. The more you see that the likenesses vastly outweigh the differences, the easier and more natural your time with her will become. For one, when you see that most of her is also in yourself you will know at once how to relate to her. Eventually you will see that you have to look long and hard to find a real difference between you and her.

Begin now to look for the many things that are almost identical in both sexes. The differences that are really there begin in the next chapter. The exercise on the next page, given with a sample reply, will help you to get the full benefit of this chapter and the next.

GUIDED EXERCISE. Find out how few gender differences there really are. Look for ways that you feel are the same for men and women and then for those that differ. When you finish there should be many more likenesses than differences.

GUIDED ANSWER. Here is how this exercise went with Bob.

Bob: So where do I start?
AFB: Try anatomy.
Bob: Should I first look for what's the same or what's different?
AFB: Your call.
Bob: Hmmm. Well, both sexes have basically the same body. You know, two arms, two legs, a head, two eyes and so on. I guess the insides, I mean the organs, are mostly the same. But women have breasts, a vagina and clitoris. Men have a penis and testicles instead.
AFB: So you feel that the basic parts are just about the same for both genders?
Bob: Yes, that's obvious. But men have more upper body strength and women are more elastic. Also, men are usually bigger and women more curvy.
AFB: Those differences build on a basic form held in common, no?
Bob: I agree. So what?
AFB: Well, if the differences begin with something held in common, then how big are they?
Bob: The physical ones are not so big, now that I think about it. I mean if I looked really close at an eye or a nose or most body parts I don't think I could tell if it was male or female.
AFB: Enough of anatomy. What about psychological differences?

Bob: Well, men feel satisfaction when they do a good job and so do women. Men can feel up and happy, or down and depressed, and so can women. Men can get angry and so can women. (pause) I'm missing something here. When I think about it, every feeling a man can have so can a woman.
AFB: How about how often they feel things and how their emotions affect them.
Bob: I think women are more emotional than men. And men are better at action.
AFB: Anything else?
Bob: (pause) Well, it seems like there should more differences but nothing comes to mind.
AFB: Who do you think does better at picking up on feelings and what they mean?
Bob: Oh, now I'm with you. Women do that better than men. No question about it.
AFB: How about how women versus men solve problems?
Bob: Let me see. (pause) Well, men are more logical and women are more intuitive.

Bob's reply to this exercise shows how a little reflection — and maybe some prodding — reveals that men and women are, for the most part, made the same way. His reply also shows how most men do not, at first, see how few differences there really are or that they come up from things held in common.

Chapter 2.

An Important Difference

She walks in Beauty, like the night
Of cloudless climes and starry skies;
And all that's best of dark and bright
Meet in her aspect and her eyes;
Thus mellowed to that tender light
Which Heaven to gaudy day denies.

...from She Walks in Beauty
by George Gordon, Lord Byron

Some men see women as an ultimate mystery. Women stand before such men as creatures of wonder holding the keys to a magical kingdom of joy and happiness. They are living promises of what can be and perhaps should be. Men follow the lines of attraction that women send out and too often find no way to connect with them at the other end. They find too little in their own masculine ways to help empathize with what women feel or value. Again and again their eyes tell them that women want them but the process of coming together miscarries. The frustrations often make women seem unreasonable and beyond comprehension.

Women's feelings on these matters are closer to men's than men usually think. Women are also frustrated, disappointed and wonder where and how to place their efforts. They have a sharper sense of where things go wrong, from their point of view, than men. That is, women are clear on where they did not get what they want and men are unclear about what went wrong in the first place. Women are usually quite specific about their discontent with men, often eager to talk about it.

I once worked with a woman, call her Sharon, whose issues make this easy to see. She was concerned about the lack of connection between herself and her lover. Their relation had a wonderful beginning. When she and Ron met they were swept along by the rush of eager feelings they gave each other and they quickly fell in love. In time the feelings subsided. Sharon realized that nature wanted them to go to the next level in their relationship. She was ready for it but her lover was lagging behind even though they were living together and sharing much of each other's life. Her unhappiness goes to the heart of the single most important difference between men and women.

Sharon: When I first met Ron I was so taken with him. He showed the kind of interest in me that a woman always wants. He seemed so together and he looked good too. He showed how he felt about me even if onlookers found it embarrassing. I miss those days. (pause) You know the rest.
AFB: Those were your glory days, when you got the kind of love that people dream about.
Sharon: Don't I know it! I'm hoping it's not over.
AFB: Is that what's on your mind?

An Important Difference 23

Sharon: When Ron used to show excitement over me I felt so connected to him. It was like he lit up because he really, really saw something good in me. He still does that and I still love it, but something is missing. Are you with me?
AFB: Yes, but I need more to make a guess at what is going on.
Sharon: I know he cares and I respect how he tries to understand that all is not right between us. But he doesn't get it. I wind up feeling alone even though he's there.
AFB: I think you're wishing that he would have more of a sense of you. Is that it?
Sharon: Sort of. I want him to know what I'm feeling. Too many of my emotions just pass him by. Every time he misses the boat I feel like I've been cheated out of getting closer to him.
AFB: So why wasn't this a problem before?
Sharon: He was always so happy to see me that for a long time I wanted nothing else but the sweet attention he gave me. He still gives it to me and I will always want that. (pause)
AFB: Something is going unsaid here. I think you are trying to tell me that he's like a person with a one size fits all way. You don't feel him moving with your changes of feeling, mood or whim. My guess is that he relates to you in basically the same way no matter what, at least most of the time.
Sharon: That's true. I don't want to lose the good things he gives me. What I want is for him to key into me more. He's like a person who sings in a monotone. If I tell him how I feel he tries to understand and then I feel like a louse because he doesn't get it. Then it happens again. My feelings change and I want to tell him where I'm at. He listens, he understands that

what I'm saying is important to me, but he just doesn't get it.
AFB: So he is content to have you there even though he is not picking up on many of your feelings. Yes?
Sharon: That's Ron. (pause) I remember what I heard a while ago. Someone said it often happens that a more emotional female, like me, will be drawn to a more logical and less emotional male. Do you remember my bringing that up?
AFB: Yes, I remember. And that mix usually works out well.

Some of the key differences between the sexes are subtle and go unnoticed. Knowing them positions you for success. Some of the less known emotional differences are connected to the striking differences in shape and form. It can easily seem that nature made women for men to admire as creatures of immense physical charm. That may be true but the way they want to be admired is a large concern for them. They have in mind a different model based on their own attraction to the charm and beauty of men's bodies. This means that a woman wants a man to cloak his physical attraction to her as much as she cloaks hers to him. It also means that a woman wants to see his emotional interest in her come first.

What's behind this is that every person wants others to see things his or her way. This is usually not egotism. It means that any one person can only see things with what nature gave him and it would be easier if others saw things the same way. A woman will want a man to look at her as she looks at him, giving her an obvious interest in her ways with a background or low key interest in her form.

The emotions of physical attraction are not entirely the same for both sexes. A man will usually feel good about being admired by a woman for his physical beauty. He takes it to mean that she is keying in to his dynamism. It is not the same for women. In the opening moments of a relation, she will resent and be hurt by a man who admires her face and form over her psychological make up, even though she wants you to be taken with her beauty. It is difficult to over emphasize the importance of the last sentence and, if some of this is new to you, it would be worthwhile for you to spend some time with the idea.

Women are beautiful and want to be seen that way. They want to feel that you as a male discover the beauty of their emotional makeup and their psyche. Only after they trust that you perceive their inner, personal beauty will they welcome your interest in their physical beauty, a thing they tend to assume from the outset. Women place considerable value on their inner experience and prize it above all else. They do not want your attraction to their lines to sideline your interest in their personalities and their ways. Most women have an almost phobic dread of being seen as no more than a sex object.

Her heart's wish is that the new man in her life will begin to learn of her inner beauty by seeing how she wears it on the outside. She wants a man to find that beauty in her expressions and how she offers them. In her eyes the magical energy of her inner world goes out to men through her form and she wants to see its effect on the man she cares about. This was the real meaning of Sharon's discontent with Ron.

Ron loved Sharon but he was missing too many of the emotions that were important to her. She had happy anticipations of how uplifted Ron would become simply by sensing how she felt. When he did not "get it" Sharon felt like he refused a gift of herself that she valued highly. Sharon's feelings were inviting Ron to draw closer to her and when he failed to respond, Sharon felt cheated twice: once for not seeing her inner beauty and once more for not taking her invitation to get closer to her.

Women see themselves as nature's most creative expression. How could it be otherwise when they are the life givers? The man who learns that a woman wants him to discover the wonders of nature within her is sure to win her immediate interest and then the happiness that only her feminine ways can bring. Women experience their inner life in poetic ways because their ability to create life makes them more aware of life itself, both its beauty and wonder. Within themselves, women do not rely on words to understand themselves or others. They use their richly intuitive feelings to understand events and to respond to them. They use their feelings to energize themselves and those they care about. The more they love the more generously they offer the gift of their feminine energy. It is very important to them that you as a male sense their energy. They want you to feel how wonderful and beautiful their emotional make up is because that is how they see themselves and that is, in fact, how nature makes them.

It is generally true that men rely more on logic and women more on intuition. The male's logical way and the female's intuitive way are both natural powers for knowing life and the world, but in different ways. Just as a male is drawn to what may appear to be a remarkable intuition in a female, so is the female drawn to the male powers of logic, focus and purpose. It is nature's design to separately express its male and female energies in different sexes. This does not mean that women are only female and men only male. Not at all. Everyone is a mixture of both sexes with one gender dominating. Women are women because female energy is dominant in them and not because there is no male energy in them, and vice versa. There is a female part to you and the more you study it the more easily you will understand women, connect with them and enjoy their company.

Women have a greatest wish when it comes to men. They wish that men will see and marvel at the radiance of their inner beauty. Women feel safe and secure when they see your male way moving with fascination from their outer beauty to their inner ways. Women are quick to trust men whom they sense want to share and enjoy how they experience themselves as women. This kind of trust is well placed because the man who can empathize with a woman's emotions must also be in touch with himself. Such a male is also more enjoyable for other men to be with because he can express male feelings that other males enjoy. This is one reason why the man who is successful with women usually has a broader appeal to other men than most.

When a woman is drawn to a man it is because she wants to experience the male voice of nature. She is aware of this. She is very much in touch with herself as the female voice and tends to assume that you have a parallel awareness of yourself. A man's inner experience emphasizes feeling the might and majesty of life and the world, and what he can do to reshape it. Women see this in men and it can easily steal their breath away or drop them in a swoon. They very much wish to draw your power closer to themselves, first to their outer beauty and then onward to their inner world where you really find them. This is a deeply sexual wish in women that completely joins their anatomy to their emotions. When you learn to see it, keep it to yourself because women want to first see the feelings they create in you before getting physical. They will delight in your sexual wish for them, even insist on it, after they see that you have eyes for their winning ways.

Women place their security within, to the inner world they value above all else and trust to guide them. They have an anxious awareness that their outer charms will fade but they see their inner self as real and enduring. They look within for a life that never stops growing, becoming richer and more complete. It is to this world, where you can marvel at the wonders of their feminine way, that they invite you and your male way.

An Important Difference

GUIDED EXERCISE. This is an important exercise for understanding the single most important difference between men and women.

Recall some lyrics that make you think of a beautiful woman. Look at what the words do to you and ask yourself what about her brings her image to you. Try to see that the lyrics bring you her image because she has so much more of what the lyrics make you feel in the first place. Now think of a actual woman who gets to you this way. In your imagination tell her what she does to you.

GUIDED ANSWER. "The Beatles' song with the words 'You've got that something...I wanna hold your hand...' really gets to me. The words say it all about what women do to me. They give me a wonderful feeling that makes me want to be with them.

"The song reminds me of a very attractive woman in my computer class. She has a certain something about her — it's hard to put into words but you can't miss it. When I talk with her, about anything at all, I get this delicious feeling. I feel a smile and an excitement come over me. The closer she gets, the more I feel this way. She must have a great deal of that good feeling herself to do this to me.

"If I told her what she does to me I'd want to use the Beatles' song. But if I had to use my own words I think I would tell her that she gives off a beautiful feeling, even though I still can't put it into words."

Chapter 3.

How Women See Men

Love me tender, love me sweet,
Never let me go.

...Sung by Elvis Presley,
from Love Me Tender [1956] by Vera Matson.

If you think that women often have a cynical view of men then you are correct. By the time of puberty women have formed an inner ideal of what a man should be like. It is rich in the feelings they want a man to give them and in the male ways they are sure will bring them joy, fun and happiness. They hold to that ideal for most, sometimes all, of their lives and they measure you against it. Just like men with women, they have negative experiences and disappointments with men and these conflict with their wished for ideal. Their outcome is more a feeling of let down with men than their giving up the ideal or even some change in it.

Many women come to admit, in confidence, that they dream of a man who is a woman in a male body. Why do they do this? They do it because they have confidence in the ability of their own gender to understand their needs and hopes. This kind of emotional understanding, that forms a basis for confidence in the other person, is very important to women. It is much more important to women than to men. Women feel instinctively that they can trust one another to empathize with their feelings and this is largely why women are so quick to fall into conversation with one another. It is also a large part of why a woman rarely spells out what she really wants from a man, for she hopes that the "right man" will key into the emotional and nonverbal things that are so important to her.

Women usually have little faith that a man — any man — can know how important their psychology is to them. They often feel that male interest is limited to satisfying sexual desire. Some women go even further and hold that men are infantile, taken up with a childish sense of power that they usually label male ego. These ideas amount to a shortfall in their understanding of how a male is made because much of what makes a male a male is the drive to change the world around him. Being male and taking decisive action go together. Being male and making plans for action also go together. Where women are more creative with what is personal, men work more with the basic raw material of life and find satisfaction by taking active measures to redefine their world. On the plus side, women expect to find this action part of their ideal with the next fellow they want to get to know. They are rarely disappointed in this hope because all men have it to one degree or another, or else they would not be male.

When a woman first meets you she feels excited by the power of your male energy. She expects this to happen and she looks forward to it. She will be looking for signs that your eyes go within her to her soul, bringing your power with them. If you are looking into her then you will feel her female energy leap out with excitement toward you; she will become unable to restrain the outflow of herself to you. However, if she is not sure that you are going within, or worse, if she feels you cannot or will not look within her, then she will pause. If she becomes convinced that your attention is not going to her inner self and personality, she will then withdraw from you with feelings of disappointment and let down.

A woman will think of you as a childish male, preoccupied with your own ego if she feels that your attention is limited to her looks and that you have little interest in her as a person. Too much interest in her sexuality and too little in her charms makes a woman feel undervalued and cheated. This is a sensitive issue with women and it makes them feel that the man who does have eyes for their person and personality is the man they want to be with.

A young woman in her late twenties, call her Gerry, was concerned about her relationships with men. She was so lovely and had such a gentle grace in her ways that I had to assume she had more than enough offers from interested men. I wondered what would concern her with all the advantages nature had given her. As she made herself comfortable it occurred to me that her likely concern was with how men treated her. Her narrative sums up much of the view from the other side.

Gerry: It's exciting to look at men and see how much stronger they are than women. The power in a man's body is a thrill to look at. That's why I don't stare at men (laughing) — I'm too proud to give away what they do to me! I admire how they like action and how much easier it seems for them to stay focused on it. It would feel so good to have that in my life. I know that most men don't know that women feel this way about them. (pause)

AFB: I agree with you.

Gerry: My work puts me in contact with people so I often meet men that interest me. I get filled with hope and excitement when I see one that looks like a good guy. I think what it would be like to get close to him and soon I'm dating him. Things begin nicely and I get lost in how nice it feels to be with him. Soon he's getting what he wants and I'm not. This keep happening and now I am concerned about how to break the cycle.

AFB: Spell out what you want.

Gerry: To begin with, I want them to see how they get to me.

AFB: Why?

Gerry: Because then they are seeing me and not just, you know, my pretty face and figure. (pause) It amazes me how a man can see that I am taken with him but not see why. Why is that so hard? I want them to have a sense of me. I know they like to be logical and to work on making life happen. But they don't see that my feelings aren't there just to please them. My feelings are important to me and I want the man in my life to know about them.

AFB: A man will take what you say to mean that it would please you if he felt your feelings more.

Gerry: That's part of it.

AFB: And the rest is about how you use them?

Gerry. My feelings tell me what things mean, what they are about. My best hunches and intuitions come

from my feelings. I get the impression that men are really in touch with their emotions, like action, sexual interest and power. But what about mine, what about what they do to him and mean to me?
AFB: You want a man who will feel your personal experience and know what it means to you, is that it?
Gerry: Every woman wants that. If all a man does is love how we make him feel, then we are left alone with things we want the man we care about to see and enjoy. It seems one sided. I can see and understand a man's way and even get carried away by it. Men don't see how women feel or use their feelings. Men see our lines, our ways and get excited over that but they don't usually make it to the inside. I want a nice guy who will share my feelings and how I find my way to him with them.
AFB: Is that your ideal?
Gerry: Sort of. I want to meet a fellow who shows a lively interest in me as a person. Oh, do I want him to find me pretty and to look forward to sex. But if he first shows some interest in me as a person and in my ways, then the whole idea of sex becomes so much more exciting.
AFB: Why is that?
Gerry: Because then making love puts him closer to knowing me and my emotions. It puts sex past just being a feel good thing to do. Women love to feel men's power during sex but we also want men to feel what we are about during sex. Isn't that what making love is supposed to do?
AFB: So the fellow who has eyes for your soul is the real turn on for you. Yes?
Gerry; Yes, that's a good way to put. That's what I want.

On first encounters women want you to find them pretty, sexy and even seductive. But they will beat a hasty retreat from you if communicate your delight over their sexuality too much. They are eager to find a male who seeks their affectionate ways and feminine energy first and their sexuality second. Women cannot resist giving you all the blessings of their sexuality if they see that you first want to enjoy what they are in themselves. Women, more than men, are creatures of their inner life. This is greater part of why the word for soul or psyche is feminine in most, if not all, languages. If you delight in her soulful ways, and what they mean to her, you will stir an irresistible drive in her to reward you with all her goodness. This is what Gerry was getting at.

Most men find a woman's way to be subtle and sometimes even mysterious. Women like the idea of you feeling this way because it tells them that you are looking at the part of themselves they most value, and most want to give you. When you key into the goodness of the real difference that makes them female they feel that they want to trust you and move toward you. Your eyes for what she is create a strong desire in her to be with you because a woman has an innate need to be seen. This is a very basic lesson that only a few men come to see and the rest spend much of their lives scratching their heads wondering what women really want.

The wish to be discovered is a very basic need in women. They see their own beauty and they are eager to enjoy giving it to the man who also sees it. The man who sees her makes her feel that it is his right to enjoy her and she instantly begins to move toward him. The man who makes her feel discovered tells her that he sees her goodness and beauty, especially the goodness and beauty she possesses behind her face and form. When a male satisfies this most basic of all female needs, she becomes lost to the wondrous feelings it gives her and all that she is wants to reward him for the blessing he gives her.

Ironically, this is a root of the cynical part of women's view of men. The need to be discovered is so deep in females that they are sensitive to even a small amount of frustration. It is difficult for a woman, who sees her beauty and that of other women so easily, to understand how a man can be so delighted with her and not understand her the way she does. At bottom, a woman assumes what she so much wants — that you can see her the way she wants to be seen as easily as she can. When disappointed this way, a woman's view of men can darken. The better outcome is that the man who discovers her is already creating love between them. Love between the sexes, for such a male, then makes him more able to discover the female because love makes each sex more like the other. This means that the male becomes more and more able to discover the female and to find ever greater joy and happiness in doing so.

GUIDED EXERCISE. Do this exercise and feel for yourself the inner experience of a woman who likes what she sees. Recall the last time you saw a woman light up over a man's attention. Picture yourself stepping into her and taking on her inner experience.

GUIDED ANSWER. Here is some narrative from a man's first try at this. Call him Bill.

AFB: This is easier for most men to do with their eyes closed.
Bill: Let me try it both ways. (pause) It's easier with my eyes closed.
AFB: Make sure you have an image of the last time you saw a woman light up over a man's attention.
Bill: That's what I have, a picture of a friend connecting with an attractive woman. How do I do the stepping in part?
AFB: Pretend that you are invisible to them from now on.
Bill: (pause) Okay, I see them but they can't see me. Now what?
AFB: Can you hear what they're saying?
Bill: Sort of
AFB: Get close enough to be able to hear what they say over any other sounds.
Bill: (pause) Okay, I'm there.
AFB: Stay there for a while. Listen to what she says and how she takes in what the man says. Pay attention to her movements, like nodding approval, pushing her hair back, smiling or standing to one side. Let me know when you can see how her expressions and movements flow with what she says or hears.
Bill: (pause) I can see the flow now.

AFB: Good. Now imagine yourself slowly getting closer to her until you begin to feel her body heat. Stop when you get there.
Bill: (pause) I feel like she is starting to blur into me.
AFB: That's good. Now take a last look at how she moves with her words and his. Let yourself go past her body boundary and blur yourself into her. Go past her body heat and step right into her. Let me know when this feels comfortable.
Bill: (pause) I'm there.
AFB: Tell me what he says and how she feels in reply.
Bill: He's smiling at her and teasing her about her freckles. That makes me, uh her, feel silly but in a nice way. It makes her laugh inside and she can feel how much he likes her. She admires him for trying his luck in public and can't hold back her smile even though she wants to. He's reaching for her hand now. I feel a rush of excitement running through her body and her breath going low. It tingles when he touches her and it's hard not to go wobbly. (pause)
AFB: What is she feeling about him?
Bill: She's hoping he won't leave yet because he's getting to her. She's looking with sweetness into his eyes and trying to tell him it's time to make plans to get together.

Chapter 4.

What Do Women Want in Relationships?

*And this maiden she lived with no other thought
Than to love and be loved by me.*

...from Annabel Lee by Edgar Allan Poe

It is true that most women are more monogamous than most men. Nature has made them this way because they are the child bearers. The male's yen to take his liberties is troubling to women and often drives them to resign themselves to the idea of never finding a completely faithful partner. Most women enter a committed relation with this kind of concern in the back of their minds, treating it as a given of the male's nature. This raises the question as to why they commit if their concern distresses them so.

Women do not want to be discovered only in the moments of your very first encounter with them. They want the process to be ongoing, and in many ways. It gives them a deep joy and satisfaction to know that you are with them in spirit and that you value what they value. At the same time, most females can be extraordinarily generous in relations. They are eager to give their lovers more of themselves emotionally than their mates are likely to. The drive to create and nourish the personality of the other, as well as the relationship, is stronger in the female than in the male. This is one root of the generosity that women so much want to give their lovers.

When a women decides to enter a relation she is certain that she can expect at least two things from it. One is that the man she cares for will continue to value and be enchanted by the beautiful differences that make her a female. She wants this more because it assures her that the relationship will grow and prosper than because she needs that kind of satisfaction — and she does need it. This may involve the male finding her mysterious at times, but that can add spice to the relation and make a woman so much more exciting to be with. The other thing she expects, and is very eager to do, is to light up his life by giving herself to his fulfillment and growth. Women are never happier than when they feel that they can fulfill the man they care about. It is their intention to give as much of themselves to this end as their lover needs and they do it with eager eyes for how it feeds the relationship. Men are not as able as women to wake up and nourish the personality of their lover. Men, by being men, satisfy a different kind of deep need in women related to how women manage their emotions. More on this later.

Women take great pleasure in how they fulfill themselves by fulfilling the one they love. This is a principle of nature that is also true of men, but it is more true of women. A woman's drive to find joy and happiness this way is so strong that it pushes what concerns she may have about her lover out of awareness and into the background. What's more, most women feel that by giving enough of themselves and their creative energy to the man they love, they will secure his love against all others. Men who do not meet women's expectation here cause women more pain than they probably know. These are events that women are not at all inclined to forget, or forgive, because they respond with feelings of deep rejection and a sense of violated trust. Their powerful sense of hurt in such a circumstance is a large part of why literature and art are so rich in material about women who have loved and lost.

Women, like men, seek a relation for the usual good things such as love, affection, emotional support, possibly a family, a shared life, and so on. However, they see these good things as ongoing events or processes rather than as goals and men see them the other way, as goals rather than ongoing events or processes. A woman feels that the good she wants will come as a result of being with a man she cares about. She also wants to feel that the good will keep coming and, trusting that it will, she chooses to give herself to him. A woman looks upon herself in a relation as a gift to the man she wants and she hopes that he will realize how she feels. Throughout the relationship she sees herself as investing her emotions to harvest a return in love or romance. The happiness she looks forward to makes her give freely of herself, and the happiness she already has with him opens her to give of herself even more generously.

Every woman has a deep hope that the man she cares for will become more and more intrigued with her personality. Women look to put men under the spell of their energy, knowing instinctively that men become intoxicated by it. One of the great goods of a relation for them is the promise that the male will ever after be charmed by her inner life. Poets and painters have known this for ages. This is why so many of the world's great work of art present women as creatures of inspired beauty, sometimes with magical power.

The next time you are at an art museum note the paintings of women made by men versus those made by women. The genders portray different aspects of what is feminine. Male artists paint the beauty, warmth and seductive charm of women. The female artists give you images of how they send sublime love to those they care for, revealing how they see themselves as givers of life. Men like to paint women as emotionally rich and women like to paint women as emotionally wise. The art of each gender expresses that gender's view of what love means to it and what it hopes love will bring.

These ideas came up with a talented man who became puzzled over what made his relation with his lover so satisfying. Call the couple Arthur and Kerry. He was something of a rigid obsessional whose underlying issue was his need to understand, and at times to control, what was happening to his feelings.

AFB: How long have you and Kerry been a couple?
Arthur: It's about eight months now. No one ever felt so right to be with.
AFB: Maybe you were never so right to feel it before.
Arthur: Could be. The strange part is that it scares me how good things are with Kerry. I enjoy her, she

is good to me, we get on well and it seems like it will continue. (pause) I can't figure why all this good news is making me anxious.
AFB: What does she do right?
Arthur: Like I said, she's good to me.
AFB: What does that mean? You like the way she makes love? She's a lively person? Spell it out.
Arthur: Of course I like her as a lover. (pause) I'm stuck.
AFB: If I asked you what seems right from moment to moment with Kerry, what would you say?
Arthur: She feels good to be with. When I hold her I get this wonderful feeling that she has a something I don't. Whatever it is, I love it! Everything feels natural and easy when I'm with her. I like to watch how she goes from one thing to the next. She can change on a dime, and with grace. That's something I can't do without getting bent out of shape. And I like how she tunes in to me. She flows almost like music in everything she does and it's beautiful to watch. Hmmm, it's like she's in touch with something that I miss.
AFB: Do have a clue to her magic?
Arthur: Aren't you supposed to make this easy for me?
AFB: You have all the pieces. Try putting them together. What connects the things you said about feeling good, music, tuning in, flowing and so on.
Arthur: There's another piece. When I miss what something means emotionally, she gets it. This happened the other day in a video we watched. (pause) The best I can say is that she understands things better on a feeling level than I do.
AFB: That's a large part of it. Do you think Kerry knows you're anxious over how good things are with her?

Arthur: I never asked myself that but I'm sure she knows. Why is this an issue?
AFB: Curious about how close you are to the answer. Kerry is emotionally rich and you are more of a head person. She knows how happy you are to be with her. She's delighted to give you such strong and welcome feelings when she knows that you and your feelings have trouble talking to each other. Your feelings are trying to tell you that she feels fulfilled by doing this to you. Your feelings are also trying to tell you that she feels certain of you because she sees that her charms are working on you, big time.
Arthur: So I'm doing something right without knowing it, no?
AFB: Yes. Your feel good reaction to her is exactly what she wants.
Arthur: That sounds too altruistic to be right.
AFB: It's not about altruism, it's about what women want. They want to see you open up because of what they do to you. That's one of the things that makes them feel the relationship will go somewhere. They're usually afraid in the back of their head that you will be fooling around with someone else or at least thinking about it too much. The more they see you come to life by what they do to you, the more certain they are of the relationship.

Both men and women see a relationship as an opportunity. On her side a woman sees it as a place to give her love in order to make things grow. What she wants to grow is mutual love and, with it, each other. She brings her heart and her heart's concern to this. Her loving wish to fulfill and be fulfilled joins with her hope that it will go on and fills her with eager energy.

Her hope to make the relationship grow and thrive makes a woman want to give herself more and more generously to the man she loves.

A woman comes to a relationship with ideas on the care and feeding of love. Her concern about its security is muted in the beginning but she knows that it will become louder as the promise of love grows. The more she gives herself and her sweet affection to love, the more her concerns grow and this makes her want to give still more. This is behind a woman's emphasis on trust in love for she does not want to feel that she is at risk in giving so much of herself. She wants love to last and she hopes that what she gives the man she loves will make him want her and what they mean to each other, more and more.

GUIDED EXERCISE. Think of a woman you would like to get to know and what a relation with her would be like. Use the stepping in visualization to discover how she feels about the relation.

GUIDED ANSWER. "There's an attractive woman in my calligraphy class. When we talk about the class she seems easy to connect with. That's more her doing than mine because she's open and enjoys fresh input from others more than I do. She seems sensitive and strong at the same time, the sort of woman I can have fun with and also get close to. I think if we became lovers that I would enjoy keying into her ways because she makes it easy to see where she is coming from. She has a way that gets to me and I think I would always feel that way about her.

"I'm visualizing myself near her to get a sense of her ways. Now I'm getting closer to her till I feel myself blur into her. And now I'm her. I can feel how much she likes the attention men give her but she's picky about who she'll date. I make her smile and she feels safe when I am nearby. She knows I'm interested in her and she wants to be with me, but she wonders if I not just out for fun and games. She would date me if she were sure I want a relationship too."

The exercise uncovers a key difference between the hopes and wishes of a man and his prospective lover. He finds that she needs to be made sure of his intentions even though he is sure of his wish for her. He can make her feel sure by simply giving her the feelings she creates in him. If he did this, it would not take long for her intuition to read his feelings and wishes, and then to see that they both want the same thing with each other.

Chapter 5.

Flirting: The First Encounter

Faint heart never won fair lady!
Nothing venture, nothing win -
Blood is thick, but water's thin -
In for a penny, in for a pound -
It's Love that makes the world go round!

...from Iolanthe by Sir William Schwenck Gilbert

Flirting is remarkably easy, much more so than most people, male or female, ever realize. At the heart of a good flirtation is a public statement that you feel good about her. Authenticity, some mirth and merriment, and feeling good about yourself all help. The key, however, to flirting is in the public announcement made by your actions that you think she is very, very nice — so nice that you risk rejection, failure and even embarrassment for her sake. Women can't help being drawn to the man who takes such action to win their interest. And the better you feel about yourself, the more they love it and feed off of it.

This is behind why most women so much like to dance. Women see dancing as a public statement on your part of how desirable and exciting you find them, and because it is public, it is socially acceptable. When you dance with a woman she takes it unconsciously to mean that you esteem yourself and are therefore trustworthy. In their eyes it takes some chutzpa for a man to be expressive in public, and especially on a dance floor. That is why it provokes trusting admiration from them.

Dancing appeals to women on other levels too. It has been called fore foreplay, and with very good reason! Dancing with a woman opens her to sexual excitement, and what better place than in public before everyone's eyes. Dancing with her relieves her of what concerns she may have over the propriety of being happy with your flirtation, or with what you do to her. True, the rhythm of the music is seductive. However, its major effect lies in the social approval of her being with you, and close to you, so soon after first meeting one another. When you dance with her you are going through an age old ritual that says you lay just claim to her and you can well believe that she sees this meaning in it, even though some of this may be unconscious.

It is tactically wise to flirt where others are present. As noted, the more you show willingness to take risks for her sake, the more she will admire you and begin to see you as trustworthy. If you are at a dance or party it is wiser to first chat with her. Dancing is a form of bonding that should follow the preliminaries of having a good initial feeling about each other. Your goals will be well served by learning to communicate to her non-verbally that you are looking for the good in her as a person. She will respond eagerly to such offerings from you and she will want very much to dance with you no matter how much of a klutz you may be on your feet. In fact, the more awkward you happen to be — while feeling good about yourself anyway — the more she will look up to you and be driven to be with you and to give you her winning ways. Women do not like men who feel sorry for themselves or who are pathetic. They crave your strength but not your "machoness" and dancing when feeling awkward is a sign of strength that will impress her and win her good feelings for you.

On first encounter they will be looking for how much they can trust in your male powers to support their emotions. This means that they see you, as a male, as having an exquisite power to make them feel more comfortable with themselves and more secure about themselves, just as they do something wonderfully chemical to your male emotions. Nature is generous and easy here. To simply offer her your interest is to excite her because she so much wants to have your male way in her life. Women do not like to make your effect on them obvious or easy for you to see, but it is there and you can count on it. Knowing that it is there and that your mere approach to her fills her with hope and sweet expectation lifts your confidence and opens you to relate to her in an easy and natural way. The ease in your approach, and the strength to carry you over the rough spots, is her first thrill with your male powers and her first taste of that exquisite something about you she so much wants.

It helps, but is not essential, to be creative when flirting. What counts, and makes for success, is letting your glee over getting a taste of her show. Being capricious and playful from a position of inner strength and confidence is very appealing to women — even to men. It's alright to be earnest but not dull because dull does not tell on your upbeat feelings about being there with her. She wants to enjoy what she does to you and it is enough to simply let your delight with her show. She wants your happy emotions and she very much hopes that she can stir even more of them in you. And so, besides thinking of what you feel you may have to do, take time to give her a chance to show you what she's got. Give her a chance to excite you more, and let her know non-verbally — with your feelings and gestures — that you are taking time out to give her an opening. She will respect you for this and that will make you more comfortable, as well as more likely to succeed.

If you see a woman who interests you in a public place, such as a store or library, take some discreet measures to make her notice your interest. No woman can resist being found attractive, especially when you make her feel that you are attracted to her winning ways. Women will respect you for being daring enough to break with convention and to approach them where it may not be strictly appropriate. And they will meet you half way as long as you continue to take the initiative in a dignified way. They will meet you half way because they are eager to find you as intriguing as you apparently find them. Women are as eager to connect as men are, but they feel that they must be cooler than men about making it obvious.

You could begin with a smile and a simple, direct statement such as "I find you very attractive" or "You're just too attractive to not approach." It pays to be honest, direct and a little daring in your delivery

Flirting: The First Encounter   53

because such qualities quickly win a woman's interest and good feelings. What's more, you can expect her eager admiration for your having the verve to try your luck with her. You can be a little more creative and in, say a supermarket, deliberately bump your carriage — gently — into hers and then comment with a smile "I'm glad you're in my way" or better "Are you in my way?". She will smile and wait for you to say something else. Say anything. It won't matter. She will be under the spell of a male who dares to take chances because he finds her so, so attractive. You can suggest playfully "I'd rather talk with you than shop" or "You're a road menace but I'll shop with you anyway." Be capricious, let your interest in her take hold of what you say, and go for it!

A good looking young man, call him Ken, was having a devil of a time connecting with women. At first I wondered what could be the matter for nature gave him the kind of face and physique that women struggle to pretend they don't see. He had a wholesome sexy way about him that women favor and a lively interest in them too. What could be missing, I wondered.

Ken described his efforts at flirting. He gave images of going to dances and like events where he would first search out the most attractive women. He would look their way and some would return his first show of interest. So far, so good. Then he related more about what he did to act on his wishes and this began to open his problem to view. Ken would look at a woman from afar and wonder what to do, and then make no further progress. I was sure he would take action if he knew what to do, but everything began and ended with looking. A little more narrative from him made his problem easy to see.

AFB: Ken, the way you describe things it sounds like you are studying women instead of flirting with them.
Ken: Well, yes, I guess it is something like that.
AFB: If all you do is look at them with a serious face, they will wonder whatever are you up to.
Ken: That makes me anxious. It feels like you're telling me that I'm working against myself.
AFB: Looking at them like objects of research is likely to make them anxious!
Ken: Really?
AFB: There are some very simple things women expect when they first meet you. I think if you add them to what you're now doing, you will soon do much better.
Ken: So what are these simple things?
AFB: The first thing a woman expects when you flirt with her is a smile. It tells her she is doing something good to you and that you like what you see. You've been standing far away, feeling a smile within yourself for how beautiful the women are, but never letting it reach your face. I think it would be a good idea to begin by making a conscious effort to wear a smile the next time.

He acted on my suggestion and returned a week later to talk about how things went.

Ken: I tried adding a smile so that I would look less like I was doing research. The women I looked at began to look at me expectantly. They never did that before. Some of them came closer to me.
AFB: They were telling you that they want to hear from you. Give a woman smile of interest and the first thing she'll want to know is what about her delights you. That's what flirting is all about. In fact, that's most of what success with women is all about.

Ken: Let me think about that for a moment. (pause) It sounds like it could be right. But even if it is, I would get stuck over what to say.
AFB: The idea, Ken, is to let your feelings do the talking. It doesn't matter at all what you say, as long as it is dignified and you put what she makes you feel into what you say.
Ken: You make it sound easy, but it isn't.
AFB: It is easy. Let me give you an exercise to show you. Recall one of those lovelies that made you smile. (pause) Now recall letting that smile come over your face. Ask yourself, if the feelings that make you smile could speak, what would they say?
Ken: (pause) My feelings are saying that she really is an eyeful and wouldn't it be nice to get to know her and wouldn't she be wonderful in my arms.
AFB: So why not bring your smile to her and let her know what it means. The thing to do is to tell her the feelings she gives you, so to speak. When you do that, you are talking in a language women understand better than men.
Ken: (pause) This makes sense. It's something I feel I can do.
AFB: Yes, you can. Just make sure to think about what you're doing before you try it. You don't want to be hasty with a simple action that will bring you more success. Play with the idea for a while before you try it. And don't expect things to come out perfect the first time.
Ken: I get the simple part. But what are you getting at about the first time?
AFB: If you tell her your feelings too literally she is likely to feel that you lack common sense and maybe even courtesy. You need to put what she makes you feel into acceptable words. You don't want to tell her

how much you would like to hold her, but you could tell her she gives off a certain something that makes you want to learn more about her. The point is that dignity is very important in your first meeting with a woman.

Ken returned one more time and reported the good news that he was beginning to see how to make it work. He was learning how to connect on his first try with new females, in at least some cases. He was wearing a smile more often and more easily, a large step for him in showing females what they mean to him.

With events like dances or parties where you are not likely to ever see a woman again, it is important to make things work the first time. This is something that needs little saying because men, far more than women, are concerned with the practical issue of when the two may meet again. Sometimes there are second and third opportunities with a woman that you want to get to know. This can occur, for example, if she happens to live near you or if she frequents the same places as you and so on. This is a time to remind yourself that persistence pays in the matter of a woman's affection. It is also a time to remind yourself that the first best approach to success with her is to let her see what she does to you.

It has often been said that a man can make a woman fall in love with him but a woman cannot do likewise with a man. This is true most of the time and points to a very important gender difference. The feminine need to be discovered and to be wanted is so basic that very often second or later attempts win a woman's interest after a few unsuccessful forays. The idea of persistence paying is true with women because they so much value your perception of them as worthwhile and beautiful. Their unspoken request that you be courteous along the way is one of the signs of how much they want you to keep making your offer, for your courtesy seasons your offer with the very sense of worth they are hoping for. If you are really taken with that lovely lady then go beyond courteous to being gracious. Such an offering will drive her to you by its high regard for what you see in her, not to mention how romantic your offering then becomes. A gracious offering makes a woman feel royal, even divine, and puts you at the center of the many romantic images that come over her. Your persistent, yet polite, interest makes a woman feel that she can trust you, and at several levels, as you will see at a later point.

The occasional need to persist has the practical implication that often a female will be quite taken with you at a first encounter, yet still hesitate about drawing close to you. This happens because most females get so little of the kind of male attention they deeply want that when it comes they feel a need to sample it again. Most females will not let you go when your first flirtation gets to them; they do not want to miss the moment any more than you do. However, some patience with females who want more can pay large dividends, for once these see that your interest is real, they will come rushing into your life with generous portions of their affections.

GUIDED EXERCISE. Think of a time when you saw a man flirt with a woman and succeed. Recall it vividly so that your image has all the details and movements. Step into the woman and take on what she sees and experiences.

GUIDED ANSWER. "She likes how he comes to her with a polite way and a warm smile. He can't keep back his eagerness to try his luck with her and she respects him for that. It makes him look strong in her eyes and she likes what that does to her. She feels good that something about her is pulling him to her. She is eager to know what he feels and she's looking at how he expresses himself to find out. He says that he likes the color of her hair and how it goes with her eyes. She doesn't care about the words but adores the affectionate longing in what he says.

"Now she is feeling anxious over whether he finds her interesting or only just pretty. She knows that he is not picking up on her concern and her smile is starting to fade on the inside. She sees him become puzzled and asks him about his work to nudge him in a positive direction. He tells her and then says he would rather know what she does. Her smile is coming back to her from within. She loves the way his interest is seeking her out in different ways. She has a good feeling about him and makes it obvious that she wants to spend time with him. But she won't give him her number until he asks."

Did the exercise seem to go too fast? Research shows that most men and women need less than about 10 seconds of eye contact to decide how attractive they find someone of the opposite sex. Some people need only about 6 seconds. This does not mean that most people are making hasty decisions. It reflects how quickly we pick up on other people's ways and how well we know our own preferences. It also means that your flirtation can succeed in a very short time.

Chapter 6.

Finesse in Flirting: The Umbrella Technique

*Night and day you are the one,
Only you beneath the moon and under the sun.*

...from Gay Divorce by Cole Albert Porter

It is in the nature of masculine ways to want to move quickly and aggressively to what a male wants. Getting to the target and winning are among the truest signs of male energy. Some men want to go faster and higher than others, and this chapter is for those men who have more of this urge than most. Much has been written about what to do after you make an initial connection — whether in your social or work life. In the social area, the real difficulty for most men is in getting started. The fact is that the majority of men would do well in relationships with the women they choose if they could only learn to succeed on first meetings. More work on flirting can quickly clear this up and open the way to more success and satisfaction.

Between the lines of the last chapter was the idea that women have certain traits in their emotional make up that they hope you will appeal to. They also hope to enjoy certain traits in you. It pays to be upbeat and to feel good about yourself. This is a good thing for yourself alone, and so much more when trying to connect with them. Women want to see your male strength and your sound regard for yourself. They also want to draw close to your energy and feel it. There are more specific ways you can do this. Two interesting chance events helped me to see what those ways are like. It was only some time later that I fully realized what they taught me. In time my understanding grew into central findings on how to succeed with women.

I was at a tennis party with a woman I was then dating. Call her Susan. Our conversation moved toward how men socialize and then she began to tease me about what a flirt I was. Not to be upstaged, I replied that my interest in women was sincere and grounded in the most healthy drives men can have. She agreed with this and drew me more deeply into how I flirt. By the way, Susan was a very accomplished flirt herself and this made the exchange all the more interesting. We began to discuss the art and science of flirting, and this was not just a tongue in cheek conversation.

I offered her the idea that she appealed to the basic need of males to be found desirable because of their strength, robustness and ability to be directed. Susan said she knew that. And then she came back at me swiftly and said "What woman would not want to be with you when you make her feel like she's the only woman in the room". The quoting is very accurate for I was so taken by the simple, sweeping accuracy of her statement that I memorized it then and there, and wrote it down as soon as I could. I knew instinctively that her spontaneous offering had a pearl of

Finesse in Flirting: The Umbrella Technique

wisdom in it and that is why I took hold of it, or perhaps I should say it took hold of me.

Take it from a woman: make her feel like the only person there and she will adore you for it. The more people there are around you, especially other women, the better. This is more than a visual technique that requires you to keep your gaze on her. You should direct your emotional interest and mental attention to her to succeed. If you are an open, expressive male and interested in her in the first place then this will come easily, and good things will then happen by themselves. Regardless of how open or expressive you are at the outset, studying the technique and looking for feedback from the woman you are flirting with you will make you better at it. It is highly effective and it feeds directly into an important part of the way they want to be appealed to. A woman will find it natural, easy and delectable to follow your energy when you treat her as if no other woman can draw your interest away from her.

Later that same year I was in Houston for a conference with two male friends. We wanted to see the sights and get a sense of the city and its people between the acts of our stay there. We sampled a number of places and were delighted to find that Houston is a friendly place to be. Everywhere we went and regardless of what we did on our first day, we found pretty women with friendly, accessible ways. The women were so lovely and inviting that we wished we could stay longer than our plans allowed. In less than a day their ways overtook us and we decided that we had to see what their company would be like.

We all set out at the same time and in the same place to try our luck. My first way is very much the directed way of males — as long as there is no indiscretion, I go for what I want when I see it with little thought for where it is or what is going on. In walking through one of the underground passages that connect the streets of Houston we came upon three gorgeous women. That was it for me! I approached them and said, with a full smile, a hearty way and the deep focus I mentioned earlier, "Excuse me. We're visitors from New Jersey and everywhere we go in Houston we just keep finding beautiful women like you. How do you do it?" Needless to say, they were thrilled and begin to meow and coo over how nice it was of us to think so and how "You really shouldn't" and "Do you really see it that way?" and "What about the gals back in New Jersey?" The only feedback we gave them was our enthusiastic smiles and eager interest. What we said counted for little because we were making the emotional offering they wanted, the kind that all women hope for.

Both groups, my friends and I as the one, the young beauties as the other, were taken with the good feelings that suddenly welled up. In a few moments we all regained our composure and we inquired about Houston in the theme of its beautiful women and their winning ways. We were sincere because these three women could only please a man's eyes, and their ways made them delightful and fun to be with. We were glad to tell them so, especially for the way they welcomed our attentions.

We walked with them — or did we float? — to a nearby coffee shop and shared a table for six. We were

Finesse in Flirting: The Umbrella Technique 65

taken by what struck us, as natives of New York City, as a wholesome beauty with a rich affectionate way. They were stuck by our obvious interest in them, and our good sense to be gentlemanly about it. All of this happened as quickly as this narrative is likely to make you guess, in just a few minutes. It worked because we keyed into them as if they were the only females in Houston and gave them our real interest in a dignified way.

The essence of this technique is to turn up the volume of the good feelings you offer a woman in a flirtation and to do it with eyes only for her. Women love your upbeat ways and your ability to channel your male strength. But they love being turned on by the delicious feelings you give them even more. A woman easily falls under the spell of a large dose of your sweet male energy offered to her and her alone. She may feel for a while that the offering comes only from you, but deep within she sees it as something she created in you. This has more to do with a woman's view of the way of her nature or purpose than with the prospect of her being narcissistic or self centered. A woman feels fulfilled, and satisfied, when she sees that a man wants to give his interest only to her and she then takes credit for what he does. It also makes her trust you because she then sees you as having the wisdom to see her worth. This is much of what women mean when they speak of being swept off their feet. At bottom, it is about a female seeing you do to her what she feels she enabled you do in the first place.

It is essential that you keep up your flow of sweet emotions to her to accomplish this. The mirth and merriment that makes this successful, and fun to do, is sure to make you brim with a smile from the very first. Your expressions should tell her in an obvious way how wonderful you feel about the opportunity to make her acquaintance. It is important that she really strikes your fancy and gives you the feelings described here. When it falls out this way you will, in part, be giving her back what she created in you all along. As noted, this is how she feels about it from the outset and she will simply adore you for giving her what she feels she created in you.

With both of these more advanced techniques — making a woman feel as though you perceive only her, and giving her a large dose of positive emotional energy — you should present yourself as a dignified gentleman. Failure to be polite and discreet will create anxiety and tension in her that you will then have to manage. It is better to optimize your chances for success from the outset by approaching her as a gentleman with courtesy and respect for her person. She will also favor your keeping in the background just how seductive and sensuous you find her. Make sure to find those qualities in her and do let your findings leak out here and there in a kind of emotional whisper. She won't fail to notice, and welcome, that you find good things about her that she would rather talk about later.

A few years later I had another experience that led to a method that made these skills easier and more fun to acquire. I was at a party looking out at the drizzle from the porch of my friend's home. A very attractive female approached the house protected by an interesting umbrella. It was made of clear plastic and came down over her to below her shoulders, surrounding her almost like a very large hat. I could see through it that she was very pretty and I was already taken with the playful spring in her step. As she approached I felt a rush of mirth come over me and I said to her "Look at this — a lady in a membrane!" She broke out in laughter and stopped in front of me waiting for more of my attention. We were soon walking together in the drizzle, sharing her umbrella. She was delightful and the experience was very satisfying, perhaps because it began with some of the high spirited teasing that most women especially like.

I worked with the image of the umbrella later on. It occurred to me that the closed space of the transparent umbrella felt like being set off alone with her, or having her all to myself, while in public. It made it easy for both of us to feel that I was perceiving only her, almost as if she and I had a great invisible bubble around us. It also came to me that the sense of enclosure that her umbrella gave fed my feeling of sending her a great deal of my personal energy. In such close, but socially acceptable quarters, we nearly touched each other and I could sense all I wanted to about her, and she about me. This makes two willing partners with an initial good feeling for each other sure to enjoy one another and also very likely to succeed!

A man who came for success coaching was taken with the idea that the umbrella technique, as I like to call it, can take hold of a woman almost instantly. Call him Tom. The idea of wrapping his attention around a woman came to him easily but he had, at first, little feeling for the sweet exuberance that women cannot say no to. The exchange, given below, shows how we came upon a way to help him get a feeling for what was eluding him. You can use what we came with up to speed up your learning too.

Tom: So it's supposed to be as simple as letting all those first good feelings go out to her?
AFB: That's a large part of it. You need to be there, as they say, giving her generous samples of your playful attention. Give her enough and she'll stay where she is waiting for more. Do it with dignity and she won't see anything but you. This comes close to hypnotizing a woman because the good feelings you create in her are what most women only dream about.
Tom: I don't think I've ever seen anything like that before.
AFB: Sure you have. The problem may be that it all happens very, very fast.
Tom: How fast?
AFB: In less than a minute, sometimes in much less than a minute.
Tom: Is there a way to see this happen, you know, sort of a demonstration?
AFB: There are plenty of actors who play the part well. Why not go to a video store and look over some titles.

He did as I suggested and returned a week later.

Tom: I found some videos with men flirting the way you said. There were some scenes with John Ritter, Alan Alda and Michael Caine that made it easy to see. Then I got curious about older flicks and Errol Flynn's reputation came to mind. I knew he was very good as a real life flirt and then I saw that he basically did what you said in his movie roles. He gave a woman a rush of sweet, smiling attention with eyes on no one

Finesse in Flirting: The Umbrella Technique 69

but her. Then I went all the way back to Valentino. I wasn't sure if a silent movie would help but his gestures showed the same idea at work. All four had that swift, generous and upbeat attention for the woman that swept her away. (pause) But these are only movies.
AFB: What about the idea of art imitating life?
Tom: What are you getting at?
AFB: The actors do their thing by exaggerating what happens in real life.
Tom: So you're saying that I should imitate them or take them as models?
AFB: That's a good starting point if you first see the basic idea in their acting.
Tom: Well, I did get the message from watching the videos. (pause) Later I began to remember places and times where I saw men flirt that way.
AFB: So how about thinking in terms of your life imitating art.

Working with Tom led to an idea that makes the learning easier for most men. Once he had emotional images he quickly got the basic idea and realized that he could do the same thing. He used it to jump start himself and learned how to make more of the connections he wanted.

It often happens when I see a woman who makes me want her company that the image of the transparent umbrella comes over me again. It makes for a pleasant rush of feeling within me that makes the event fun and exciting, as well as easier and more effective. Bring the umbrella technique with you into the exercise below and then into your social life. Keep in mind that the imagery helps you to give her the kind of attention she very much wants. It also gives you the upbeat and happy feelings that work well in first encounters. You can work later on being mindful of the important point, already made several times, that her nature makes her see the good things you give her as her handiwork.

Finesse in Flirting: The Umbrella Technique 71

GUIDED EXERCISE. Recall a woman you would like to get to know, someone you have not yet flirted with. Visualize yourself using the material of this chapter to make a successful connection with her.

GUIDED ANSWER. The dialogue below shows a young man, call him Matthew, learning to use these ideas. It begins after he has chosen an image of a woman he wishes to connect with.

AFB: Imagine that it's Spring time. It's raining lightly and both of you are sheltered beneath a clear, plastic umbrella. You can see dreamy, impressionistic images through the water running over the umbrella, but others cannot see in. What does the image do to you?
Matthew: I feel like I have her all to myself and that makes it easier to talk with her. She is smiling eagerly, as if she likes what's happening. I feel a big smile coming to me because she's so close and seems to like it, but I want to stifle it.
AFB: Give her your smile and your attention. She wants to see what she does to you and to feel that she has all your attention.
Matthew: I'm looking at her as we walk in the drizzle. I'm telling her how much I like walking in the rain as long as there is no lightning. She laughs and says she feels the same way. I can see her step becoming more lively all of a sudden. I feel good about this but I no longer know what to say.
AFB: She's the woman you want and she is inches from you. You have her all to yourself and no one can see you. What does this do to you?
Matthew: She's special. I love the way she looks. I feel that she has so much life and fun in her.

AFB: Find words for your feelings and give them to her.
Matthew: That sounds like something a poet would do.
AFB: Tell her how she makes you feel by expressing the sweet things she does to you. The words don't matter. It's all in the delivery. Be generous with your interest in her and lighthearted.
Matthew: (pause) I'm telling her how much I like the way the rain makes the ground smell. It brings up the smell of the soil and reminds me of the sprouts and flowers that will come later. She likes hearing this. I'm telling her that the Spring rain makes me feel like having fun. That lights her up and she's giving off a lot of good feelings. I think I'm making myself really obvious.
AFB: That's why you're getting her best feelings. She wants to see what she does to you. Let your smile come to you because its her proof that you are taken with her.
Matthew: She's saying that Spring brings out new and fresh feelings and not just flowers. (pause) I don't think I should tell her just yet how I feel about her, not that she doesn't know! Now I'm telling her about beautiful gardens nearby that we can go to and see the things we are talking about. She says she likes the idea.

This is a very useful exercise. Play with it by tailoring it to a woman whom you want to get to know. Do it until you master the material behind it and you will find yourself spontaneously giving women the expressions and the kind of attention they are always hoping for.

Chapter 7.

Getting to Know Her

*The meeting of two personalities is like
the contact of two chemical substances:
if there is any reaction, both are transformed.*

...from Modern Man in Search of a Soul
by C. G. Jung

    Successful flirting opens the door to a relation and this leads to many other possibilities for fun, fulfillment and growth. The opening phase of a relation offers an opportunity for that romantic excitement that makes all the world gladly step aside with a smile. It is a time of emotional magic, filled with the wonder of finding each other and feeding off of each other. True, it is transitory, but few things in life are as rich in excitement, pleasure and adventure. The great good awaiting you in getting to know her makes this a time to be studied and savored.

    If she wants to get to know you then she already has only the best in mind for you. She wants to see how much she can share her inner, emotional world with you and how much you enjoy being close to how she experiences herself. Sharing the wonder that she feels within herself is, in her eyes, the major good she has to give you and she is eager to do so. Sexual relations for her are your opportunity to enter more deeply into her as a person. Most females beyond adolescence will warm to the idea of making love only after they feel sure that doing so will draw you closer to them as persons. It is an event of great trust on her part to give you herself sexually because she sees this as a special gift, one that she will not offer lightly. When a woman offers her intimacy to someone new she feels she is taking a risk and, in the back of her mind, she is hoping for the best.

Traditional gestures such as gifts of flowers or perfume tell her more than that you find her special. She will see these tokens as your way of telling her that you sense the magic of her feminine ways and their energy, and that you are overjoyed with what you find. Inwardly, she will take this to mean that you welcome the invitation of her affection and tenderness to awaken you to more of yourself and to a richer experience of yourself. This is an area where she knows that she has both a great gift of nature and a commanding lead over men. Most women are careful to offer just enough of a small dose of their enchanting differences to make a man want more. They are concerned that too large a sample of it may make him feel that she is overwhelming. A woman enjoys waiting for the right moment to charm him with more and this is one root of the remarkable patience most women have — when it comes to the men they want.

Getting to know each other in the honeymoon phase is mostly about learning to be inspired and uplifted by each other's emotional life. The more you see and feel her actual beauty as a person the more successful the relation will be; you will also enjoy her more and find yourself energized by what you do together. When you are being natural this will happen by itself without any further effort on your part. If you find yourself struggling to see these things then you probably have not selected a woman who is right for you, at least for now. It would then be a good idea to look closely at how well you work and play together and how well she fits your wishes, needs and hopes.

If the choice is right then you will find yourselves feeding off of each other. You will find her interesting, sexy, creative and fun to be with. You will look to her for inspiration and support in the emotional parts of your own life because her intuition finds these things more easily and more clearly than most men can. She will seek and find security in your greater male willingness to take chances and your greater ability to focus your energy. You will naturally select different areas for leadership with each other and you will both be happy with those choices. Joint leadership will arise in those many areas where the sexual difference vanishes, that is, in most parts of your experience of each other. If she cares about you then you can expect her to be eager to take an emotional lead, lifting your spirits higher and surprising you with a remarkable sense of what things means emotionally, not to mention her endless glee with life itself.

A lively young woman, call her Amy, was having comic problems with a fellow, Jason, she had just begun to date. The issue was getting Amy to see that Jason wanted her to take charge, at least some of the time, while getting to know each other.

Amy: I really like the new man in my life. Jason is fun to date, has a great sense of humor and loves adventure. I'll do things with him I would not do alone or even with most men I date.
AFB: That's the good news.
Amy: Right. He's bright and perceptive too. But there are things he doesn't get. I'm a woman. That means I'm a leg up on him psychologically, just like he is with his daring ways. (pause) I really like those ways! It feels so right to be with him, uh, most of the time. But some times I feel like I want to hit him on the head with a frying pan! (pause)
AFB: Let me guess what's going on. He wants to be in charge all the time, even when it doesn't fit. Yes?
Amy: Jason is a really nice guy and it's easy to see that he likes how I make him feel. And I like the way he makes me feel! Things are great when we're doing something I would be too cautious or just plain scared to do myself. Then he feels in charge. (pause) He should be in charge then because I don't know up from down about being daring. But then we'll go to dinner someplace nice. Our feelings go to each other and I can see how he feels. When we get up to dance I feel like inviting him to me and I know he wants that. But he becomes a blockhead the way he stifles his feelings.
AFB: But he still gets close to you and satisfies your need for affection?
Amy: No problem there. It's getting him to open up. If we go to a movie and talk about it he avoids talking about the feeling part. If I can enjoy following him in being more daring why can't he follow me in being more emotional? I know he cares but he's frustrating me here.
AFB: I think he is open to the feeling side of things. How else could he satisfy you?

Getting to Know Her 77

Amy: (pause) Let me put it differently. Jason can be tender and sweet. But his idea that he should always be in charge is not going to work.
AFB: It sounds like it's working now.
Amy: It's early in the relation. I'm still thrilled with all his pluses. It's just a question of time before I'll put my foot down and tell him how I feel.
AFB: You like what you see in him even though he likes to play general. And he likes what he finds in you. So the problem is...?
Amy: What about what comes naturally to me?
AFB: It looks like you have a good thing here and I think he already knows how you feel. In fact, I have a hunch he's waiting for a show of strength from you to set things right.
Amy: I never thought of that.
AFB: Your frustration is getting in your way. You need to get past it for a balanced view of things. Then you can sock it to him.
Amy: I bet he would like that!
AFB: People who are too much in charge usually want someone else to take some control away from them. If you take the emotional lead the way you want to, I bet he'll adore you for it and follow at once.
Amy: That would make the relation more balanced.

Poets have recognized for centuries that nature expresses something extraordinarily beautiful in women. Poets like to call that beauty, and its power, the eternal feminine. They have spun the idea in rhymes and lyrics and have been faithful to what that beauty is and what it does. As you move into and past the honeymoon phase you will know if this remarkable beauty in her is touching you. How will you know?

You will be taken with her. You will be taken because it is difficult to stop your inner life from leaping out of you to meet the offer of what she is and to enjoy the happiness that her winning ways promise you. It may even happen big time, as the expression goes, and you will then find yourself in love with her.

Love is one of the natural and healthy outcomes of a male seeing this wonder, the eternal feminine, in a woman. Women know this better than most men do and that is one reason why women are so, so good at waiting. They know deep within that there is a very good chance you will eventually be smitten by what they know they have within themselves. And they are unwilling to let on that you have gotten to them first because their need to be discovered by you means more to them than letting you know how they feel about you.

If finding love is not your objective now then you should probably take time out to think over what you want. If your current interest is to enjoy life or to have more fun with little prospect of commitment then keep in mind what nature might have in store for you. Falling in love can simply take a hold of you, as if coming from nowhere. This happens when you are ready for it and cannot happen otherwise. This means that when you find someone who is right for you, she will flood you with the best feelings life has to offer. This will happen whether or not you think you are ready because your deep inner nature knows better when you are truly ready and this marvelous part of you will not let you miss an opportunity for so much happiness.

If now is not the time for a committed relation then it simply won't happen, even if you consciously want it to. Nature cannot smite you with the overwhelming power of love when you have more important needs elsewhere. Falling in love presupposes being ready for love. You may have no more than a healthy need to sample different personalities while learning more about females, and life in general. If this is what your energy feels like doing then follow it by taking your time and enjoying yourself. It is close to inevitable that at some later time a lovely female will captivate you. When you meet her she will leave you little choice but to welcome the wonderful things she does to you, and make you feel that the only good thing to do, the only wise thing to do, is to be with her.

Many people who are ready for love do not realize it and most people who seek love over enjoying their social life fail to find the love they want. The first are often swept away by joyful, even intoxicating, feelings that they only later come to recognize as love. The second often fail to learn how to enjoy the preliminaries before going for the main event. Trying to run before they can walk, they never master walking, so to speak. Getting to know her is an important kind of fun that love wants you to have before a deeper relation begins. In fact, if you don't have fun, love will not even try to enter because love wants to have a place prepared for it by how you relish each other.

GUIDED EXERCISE. Find out what you're looking for in dating and relationships. Visualize someone you would like to meet and get to know. Imagine that you are dating her and watch where the movie in your mind goes.

GUIDED ANSWER. "I have a new neighbor and she is so cute! I try not to stare at her, but I have to because I want to see if she's interested. It takes just a few seconds for my mind to see us together. I'd love to go roller blading with her in the local parks, and now I'm doing that with her in my mind. We feel the air run over us and ogle each other in motion. We stop by the falls for a while to eat a lunch we packed. We're all eyes for each other and we have to shout over the sound of the waterfalls to hear each other. Next we go to see a movie and then it's pizza and wine on the living room floor. We eat from the same slice of pizza, starting at different ends. What a meeting in the middle!"

It did not take this fellow long to realize that having fun was more important to him than finding the love of his life. The next time a pretty lady makes you forget everything else, let your mind run free with her and find out what you really want.

Chapter 8.

Endings and Beginnings

No sooner met, but they looked;
no sooner looked but they loved;
no sooner loved but they sighed;
no sooner sighed but they asked one another the reason;
no sooner knew the reason they sought the remedy.

...from As You Like It by William Shakespeare

The end of a relation is not one of life's most welcome events, even when there are many good times to look back on. There is an up side to ending in the opportunity it offers you to do better than ever before. However it ended, there is a harvest of emotional power and usable insight in why it ended. The discontent that brought it down contains seeds for more and better the next time. When properly managed, endings are also a time for you to learn how to make yourself more desirable to women than ever before.

The hurt or emotional upset that you are likely to feel when you and she are no longer a couple can hold you up. It is therefore wise to first deal with that hurt or upset. Where there is hurt there is anger, as well as other negative feelings. It is a good idea to wait for the negative emotions to simmer down and then to call or write her. You will know that the time for this action is right by the return of good memories of her over hurtful or frustrating ones. Let her know that although the relationship is over, she gave you good things that you will cherish. Remind her of how you prospered together and of the joys that you shared. Let her know that you will carry these good images with you as you go forward. She will want to hear this for several reasons and it will do you good for even more.

A woman does not want to feel that she has so hurt you as to anger you or impair you. It will relieve her to know that you are in good spirits and moving on, rather than seething with resentment or languishing in pain. Your news will make her feel that she has no need or reason to feel guilty over the outcome. She also will respect and admire you for communicating good will to her as well as your intent to pursue a happy, rewarding life. She will bring these good feelings for you into her life and this can only work for well in yours. At the very least knowing that a former lover has good feelings for you will lift your mood and self esteem. Her good feelings will energize you to pursue more good things in life and make you feel freer to relish them than you otherwise would.

It is important to sincerely feel this way toward her. Why do this, you may wonder, if it is unlikely that you will have much more contact with her? There are many reasons to do so. Women do not want to pity men. If a new woman in your life senses or actually knows that another woman pities you, it is not likely to work toward your success with the new one. They

Endings and Beginnings   83

want to admire men who rise above their wounds; they see this as expressing the power of your masculine energy. The sight of it fills them with images of valor that they feel they have found in you. Women love to find heroic ideals in men and, finding such a man, they want to give themselves to him.

You will also want to go forward in your life with an assuring inner sense that she supports you as a person and wants you have a happy, satisfying life. Calling or writing her first, as suggested above, will help to create this. Knowing that her good wishes go with you will create a seductive energy within you that will promote more success. This energy is a positive emotion that women easily see and respond well to. It attracts them by making them feel that you are a man of strength and high purpose whom they can admire and trust. Much of this attraction to you comes from women sensing that you have managed the end of a relation in a way they can only admire. This will also make a woman want to be the next one in your life as a successful rival over your last love, whom she will regard as passing a good thing by.

The feeling that your aftermath with your former lover has the support of your next one will improve your mood and energize you. Your next lover will also want things to turn out this way. She will want you to bring a high regard for your prior love into your life and she will very much respect you for doing so, for your next love will want to feel that she is of even greater value than your last. As for your former lover, there is more here than her self esteem and her need for your good will. There is also the practical issue of how the baggage of emotional resentment can interfere with your enjoying and getting to know the next female in your life.

The next woman you meet will intuitively sense how your last relation ended. That next woman will want to see higher values and some ideals in what she senses. She will want to respect and admire that you released each other from your involvement in a gracious way and with good wishes for one other. By ending with good will and mutual support you gain more than making your life easier in all that you do; you also build within yourself the trustworthiness that women so much want to see in men. Trustworthiness affects women like the heroic ideals and valor they simply adore finding in men. All these images make women want to be with you, to feed off of you and to give themselves to you.

When you look back at what you had with her, you can only account for yourself. This means that you can only be sure of how it felt to you and what did not work for you. You can only speculate as to how she feels about it. Short of looking her up and asking, there is no way to remove the uncertainty you have over just how she feels about your time together. There is a positive side to your uncertainty over her view of things because exploring it can be your opportunity to make major gains in how to succeed.

Try to look back on the relation from her point of view as a woman and to see what she wanted or hoped for but did not find. It can help a great deal to talk this out with a female friend, not someone you are romantically interested in. Did you, for example, come to a point where you no longer found her person and her ways engaging and beautiful? Are these signs of this, the most hurtful of all outcomes on her side? If there are then you will do better by keying more into your next lover's make up or finding a next lover with whom this feels more natural. Did she end up feeling that she could not inspire you or effectively support your hopes? If so, you may do better with a more vibrant or a more expressive woman. The shoe could be on the other foot here, if she found you too needy. In this case you may want to get to work on becoming more self reliant and discovering more of your own powers.

Both of these female wishes — to have a male discover the many kinds of beauty nature has given her and to emotionally support and inspire the man she cares for — are of fundamental importance to women. They see both of them as gifts of immense value to you, and this is true even though the flow of attention differs from one to the other. The first wish has you looking at her and beholding her, but her second wish has her giving herself to you in an emotionally intimate way. You can make large gains in your next success by studying your last relationship for signs of a shortfall with either of these female wishes. You can motivate yourself to do this by noting that when it comes to a woman's affection, it really is true that the more you give, the more you get. It can only be a woman's way to return more because she sees what you give her as a thing she inspired you to do. She then feels satisfied with her own good work with you and wants to do more.

A likable and business-like young man, call him Roger, felt he was carrying a torch for his last love.

He is an example of how a man can break free and jump start himself for more success once he understands what was amiss in his last relation.

Roger: So maybe Linda was the one great love of my life.
AFB: Why do you say that?
Roger: I can't think of anything but her. It's been a few months and I still keep cycling back to her in my thoughts.
AFB: What was so right about her?
Roger: (pause) We had a lot in common. We understood each other, we shared the same interests and we were good as lovers. (pause)
AFB: What was exciting about the relationship?
Roger: Huh?
AFB: You gave an intellectual description of your relation. Where did you two have passion?
Roger: Well, we really liked being with each other. (pause)
AFB: Tell me, Roger, what did Linda do to energize you?
Roger: I don't know what that means.
AFB: Did she have a way about her that make you feel really, really up? Did she have a way that made you feel like you can't wait to be with her again?
Roger: Why, no, we never were like with each other.
AFB: Sounds like you had an arrangement, not a relation.
Roger: Huh?
AFB: A guy and a gal form a relationship to turn each other on with emotional excitement. She should light your fire, as they say, and you should light hers.
Roger: That sounds like stuff you read about or see in the movies.

AFB: It sounds like neither of you ever met someone who got to you. Was there ever a woman in your life who made you get carried away with sweet feelings?
Roger: No.
AFB: Did Linda ever talk that way about anyone in her life?
Roger: No.
AFB: Then why do you miss her so?
Roger: Because it felt right with her.
AFB: Suppose you met someone who gave you such a good feeling that you would take the day off just to be with her. Suppose she made you so happy that you looked forward all day to being with her again. What would happen to Linda then?
Roger: This is all make believe.
AFB: Very well, make believe it's happening. What becomes of Linda?
Roger: Who's Linda? (pause) Can women really do that?
AFB: You said it's all make believe. Why not try a few movies that portray a man being star struck by a woman. Put your disbelief on hold and let the story get to you.
Roger: What does this have to do with Linda?
AFB: Both of you needed the same thing, someone to energize the relationship. You'll forget Linda as soon as you see that you need a lively, expressive and colorful female in your life. A woman like that will enjoy lighting you up and, on her end, she'll feel better put together for being near your male ways.

There are other ways the relation may have fallen short. Perhaps she felt that you were not as proud of her as a person as she wanted. Women very much want you to see their worth as persons. This is one core issue where men and women are very similar, though the meaning of high esteem differs from male to female. When you fail to acknowledge a woman's worth as a person, she is likely to see you as sexist and become anxious that your esteem for her is poorly grounded. The female need to be regarded with pride is much, much older than feminism, though the latter has given the need a new wrinkle or two. Women know that nature has given them, more than men, certain remarkable ways and powers. Their sense of worth, and their wish for your pride in them, has its deepest roots in those ways and powers. Showing less pride in her than she wants also risks your not enjoying what she has to offer as much as you could, and this is something she will know before you.

You will know when your look back has brought you to the real issues. A sense of conviction and an "aha" feeling will come over you, telling you that you are going in the right direction. That "aha" feeling grows to a crescendo as you come to root insights into why you gave up the relationship. These discoveries are valuable because they show you how to do better next time. Each discovery is both a success lesson and a gain in your own personality because you cannot become better at doing what works without also becoming more evolved as a person. The latter is one of many reasons why endings can lead to fresh beginnings with more promise.

You may be tempted to call your former lover when you feel you have found what the problems were and to discuss them with her. The temptation to share an important insight with someone you cared about can be compelling and the motives can be commendable. It is usually not wise to call and discuss your findings, unless you have a strong sense that you now know how to make the relationship work and want to resume it. Discussing your insights with her carries a downside risk. She could easily feel that things would have turned out differently if she had given more of herself, or had been more in ways she still struggles to understand but fails to find. Why risk hurting someone you shared an important part of your life with, unless you have some worthwhile and compelling reason? She may be profiting as much or more than you from work on her end in the same spirit as your own. It is generally better to keep your new wisdom to yourself and to use it for happier and more effective actions as you look to life for a new love.

GUIDED EXERCISE. Play your last relationship in your imagination from beginning to end, until you see why it ended. Use what you find to make a better choice next time.

GUIDED ANSWER. "Shirley was a lot of fun to be with. It lasted about six months. I remember meeting her at a friend's party and how her perky ways got to me. We went for a picnic down by the bay, broke out our skates and tried to skate in the sand! We fell in the water and got closer than we should have on a first date. She was a high energy person, lots of fun to be with and willing to try most anything. She lived just a few miles away so it didn't take long for us to be spending week nights together, at her place or mine. Weekends together were a given.

"We went to a lot of parties together and people picked up on how much fun we had together. It wasn't just dancing, it was more the way we would play with each other and feed off of each other. It went on like this for many months. Then it slowly became harder and harder to make time for each other. She would cancel out on me, but I would cancel out on her too.

"Now that I think of it she made it harder to continue than I did. I don't think either one of us wanted to do more than have fun. She got tired of it before I did and I think that's why she was first to begin to thin out our time together. I miss her and I would date her if she called. But I still want to have fun and I don't plan to be alone. I guess the bottom line is that we were playing games with each other and she was better at it than I was."

This man realized that his last relation ended because he was in a phase of life where his major need was to enjoy himself and otherwise be free. He made a good choice of a playmate with Shirley and was enough of a good sport to credit her with playing his game better than he did.

Chapter 9.

Starting Fresh

I've taken my fun where I've found it

...from The Ladies by Rudyard Kipling

If you are not in a relation now then chances are you're looking for the next female to brighten your life. It is usually not a good idea to rush from one relation to another. Take some time to gather up a yield from your last one, as outlined in the last chapter. Reaping your rewards this way can take anywhere from a few weeks to several months, depending on how deeply involved you were. Gathering a yield is well worth your time because it will make you more ready than ever for success in love. Also, you will become ready for your next love sooner with a harvest than otherwise.

There are a number of ways of knowing when you are at a good time to find someone new to enjoy. You may simply see what your last relation taught you about doing better next time and decide to go ahead and make it happen. When the aftermath takes place more below awareness than in it, there are other signs to look for. Nature will first try to tell you that you are ready for a next romance by piquing you with a restless energy and an eagerness for fresh excitement in your life. If these things fail as your wake up call, then you can count on your chemistry to loudly tell you it's time to go shopping for a new lady to upgrade your life. This is usually nature's last signal and it always works because nature can turn up the volume as much as needed to get your attention.

The expression, never say never, has its place here. It is not always a good idea to not move quickly from one relation to another. If your major wishes and needs are to have fun and to experiment with life then not moving quickly to a next relation will work against what is good for you. The need to enjoy learning social skills and more about yourself is healthy, necessary and worthwhile. By no means should you deny yourself this pleasure. This is usually truer of younger males than older, but a male of any age can be in a life situation where having fun is the best thing to do.

One key to more success is to not only want more from your next relation, but to demand it. This demand should rise up from within yourself and not be directed at the next female that enchants you. It is more of an attitude toward life about giving you what you deserve. Highly successful people are quick to say that you have to make life pay your price. Take their advice seriously because every part of life tends to give you as much as you feel entitled to, and your sense of entitlement tends to create the will and the way to get what you want. If your last relation gave you less than you wanted, then insist that life bring you more and better next time. The deeper and more authentic your sense of entitlement, the faster you will see and attract what you want.

Making the move to starting fresh is best done by putting together your various gains. This means, for example, that you will enjoy the greatest increase in your success by adding what you have learned from your last romance to your demand for more from life and to a deeper sense of entitlement. Spend some time with the transition from working through your last relationship to actively looking for a new one. Reminisce on your last love and the ones before her, so that you may study and learn from them. Let the images tell you things about your emotional responses to your former loves that escaped you when you were with them.

Ask yourself what kind of women were you drawn to. Do they feel so right for you that you would want to find the same kind of lovers again? If the answer is yes, then make sure you are choosing well rather than repeating a poor choice. It is not easy to decide this question by yourself, especially if you have blind spots for some of the good things a relation can offer. When the answer is yes, you may want to seek out a female friend as suggested below to make sure that you have not been shortchanging yourself.

If finding the same kind of lovers again does not appeal to you, then there is more to consider. For one, why did your prior relationships not work out to your satisfaction? What frustrated your wishes and made your fondest hopes elude you? What in your coming together left a bad taste in your mouth? The answers to questions like these will tell you to be wary of women who give you a certain feeling, found in the images you relive. That telltale feeling will spare you wasted time, effort and false hope by serving as a protective warning from within yourself.

There is no single reply to this kind of questioning and here you have to do your own research. This is not something needing the help of a therapist. It can be enough to talk about it with a female friend, one who does not know your former lover. Such a friend will be motivated by her innate sense of rivalry with your former lover to tell you what was amiss on your lover's side; and her judgment will not be clouded by sympathy for your last love. A friend who knows your former lover will be more likely to tell you what you could have done better. In both cases, you are likely to find that female friends will quickly see things of great value that you don't. They will admire you for asking such questions of them and be eager to help you, even the ones who may want to be the next love in your life. Women cannot do anything but admire a man who inquires about their make up, and this is so true it can well be called a law of female nature.

It is true that no one thing answers to all the questions coming from a look back. However, there is a universal gain in doing so before starting fresh. Your recollection of what happened can tell you valuable things about yourself, especially what it is about you that women want. Your recall of former lovers can make you see more clearly that you already have what women want. This applies to all the women who ever loved you, whatever the mix of satisfaction and disappointment you had with them. You have a certain something as a male that women want and that is why your romances began in the first place. The idea is to use prior experiences with women to get more in touch with what that certain something is. This happened with a young man of many interests, call him Steve.

Steve: It's been a few months since things ended with April. She was as pretty as her name. We spent about a year together, having good times and getting close to each other. Now I'm starting to see what went wrong even though so much felt so right with her. (pause) I run in a lot of directions. I like to do a lot of different things. She was very colorful and warm but that warmth turned out to be more of a domestic thing.
AFB: So eventually it came down to her getting tired of doing things that she really didn't want to do for your sake. And on your end, you got tired of trying to be a couch potato.
Steve: Well she's not exactly a couch potato but that's about right. There's more. April would often get lost in her feelings. This never bothered me because she was so colorful and had such high energy. (pause) I'm getting stuck here and I don't know why.
AFB: When her feelings carried her away maybe she wanted you to pull her back in. Is that it?
Steve: I felt like she was reaching out to me to do something and I didn't know what it was.
AFB: Did you ever ask her?
Steve: No, I was afraid of hurting her feelings. No, that's not really true. I never asked her because I was afraid of what she might say.
AFB: Like what?
Steve: Like what you said. I was supposed to crawl under her skin and take charge of her runaway feelings.

AFB: That's a strong statement. Are you sure of this?
Steve: Yes. Why do you ask?
AFB: Because you're showing the kind of anxiety that goes with a wish like that from a woman. I wanted to see how much you connect your anxiety with her need.
Steve: Oh, I see it! I just don't want to deal with it in a relationship.
AFB: Let's deal with the good part. What drew you to April?
Steve: Well, she really is good looking and has an elegant way. Then when I first spoke with her it felt like I stepped into a rainbow of good feelings. We connected very quickly.
AFB: What did she connect with in you?
Steve: I don't know.
AFB: Yes you do.
Steve: Oh, you mean the thing that made anxious?
AFB: Yes.
Steve: Well, I didn't know at first what she saw in me. As we got to doing things I enjoyed how much she liked to get close, almost wrapping herself around me. After a couple of months it began to feel sort of clingy. Then I started to feel that she saw me as having some kind of strength and I couldn't figure out what it was. This confused me because I don't see myself as such a strong person.
AFB: I believe you were picking up on how you she looked to your steady ways to make her feel more centered.
Steve: That fits. Her emotions are colorful but they're overdone. It would have worked better if she didn't want me to rope her back in so much.

The rest of the exchange was about how other women, who are not as emotionally diffuse as April, also look to men to make them feel more centered. This part of a relationship gives a woman a great deal of joy and satisfaction. It makes her feel proud of her lover for having so much of what she wishes for and for offering it to her in a tender way. The male way has a universal appeal to women because it is a part of nature given more to men than women. In other words, women can't do without it and feel complete at the same time. This gives men a power over women that women are very aware of but unwilling to reveal — to men. Women know, and relish, that the male way can undo them and leave them feeling that they can only follow what it does to them. Most men do not know they have this power, but it is there in every male waiting to command female interest.

The exchange with Steve shows how a male's directed way and power to hold to his course appeals to a woman's emotions. It also shows how a woman's emotions can tend to go their own way within her, at times almost with a life of their own. This was more true of April than most women, yet it remains true of women in general. These are two of the few real differences between the genders that draw men and women to each other. And, yes, a woman's position in her cycle does affect how easily her feelings can roam free within her.

There is more to learn from your recent past about charting a better course before looking for the next female to beguile you. Compare how you experience life now, after your last love, with how it was before you met her. Perhaps she had more of a flair for calling people's motives than you and you became her understudy, rising in your sense of what moves people. Perhaps you had a better sense of form and organization than she and now she sees how things come together better than before she knew you. When two people care about each other and share a part of their life, they literally become more like each other, even if they eventually go separate ways. Seeing how you and your last love enriched one other will bring you many gains. Such understanding will make you even more attractive, if not seductive, to the kind of females that can give you the most joy and satisfaction. It will help you to make better choices of lovers and will make successful connections with them come more easily to you.

Every gain in seeing where you, as a male, are ahead of most women will make it easier for you to relate to them. Such awareness will tell you what part of your person they most want you to give them and how to deliver it. Each time you see where women are ahead of most men will help you in a number of ways. This kind of awareness will show you where to value them more highly, as they so much want you to, and will also make you want to do so. You will learn how to enjoy them more and then see special things about them that they want you to adulate. Those special things will almost always be a part of their intuitive beauty and how they cherish it. For example, you may suddenly realize that your former lover knew your best feelings for her long before you did, even though you felt you had to "let her know."

Finding more of the places where men and women are very much like each other turns up a yield of another kind. This positions you to see where you can relate to her as you would to almost anyone else, a point discussed earlier. Your next effort with a female whose charms pull you her way will feel easier and more natural when you see how much like yourself she is. However, she will hope to see the contrast of an important difference in the way you relate to her. The important difference she wants is the one between how you give yourself to her over someone else. The difference she hopes for will lie in her wish that you treat her feminine beauty and power as things you have not seen before or see more of in her than ever before.

The next woman who wants you in her life will be continuous with the last one. If she cares about you then she will want to help you with any emotional carry over from your last relation. In time your next love will help you to finish working through your last one. She will do this more with loving care for you than with a sense of competition with the one you left behind, for she will instinctively see your last lover as a rival over whom she is already victorious. The work you do together on you will draw you closer and deepen your understanding of yourself, of each other and of women in general. It will also teach you more about what is important to love itself, as a third thing coming from the two of you. This means that you will see more of how to grow a happy and satisfying relationship.

As noted, placing trust in their mate is a larger issue with women than men and that will surely be true of the next woman in your life. Sharing your inner experiences with her will deepen her trust. If you want to understand more of yourself, or of her, then just tell her. She will be eager to help you because her feminine make up is closer to the intuitive meaning of the psyche than your male make up. She will also like helping you simply because she is a woman and her nature is eager to cooperate and to be supportive. She will feel good about your openness and interpret it as accepting more of your feminine side, as well as getting closer to the magic of her own way.

In time she will want to learn more about the male principle through you. Women look upon it as a mystery of such enchantment that they approach it slowly, respecting how easily it can make them its willing captive. Women are endlessly curious about how it feels to be a man because they know what men can do to them with a power their gender has less of. As her trust in you deepens she will want you to share more and more of your inner experience as a male. This will make her more like you and her invitation to you will make you more like her.

GUIDED EXERCISE. Find something you want more of from your next relation. Look to your last relation to see what kind of female can satisfy you more than the last one and what you can do to make it happen.

GUIDED ANSWER. Here is some narrative from a man, call him Ted, whom I helped reply to this.

Ted: I'd like to have more of a say in my next relation. Barbara was good to me but I usually felt like she ignored my input when we were together.
AFB: Is this about the things you would do together or about how it felt to be with her from moment to moment?
Ted: She was open to what we would do, about times and places and things like that. It was more how she made me feel. (pause) I guess she was a control freak. I never felt like I had much of a say about things with her.
AFB: If she was open to what you did together, then how could she make you feel this way?
Ted; Well, she was controlling, like I just said.
AFB: It sounds more like the issue was your shyness to say what was on your mind than her taking charge.
Ted: So you're saying I should have spoken up more?
AFB: It's probably both. She does sound like she enjoys running the show emotionally and you seem to be reticent about expressing the feelings that are important to you.
Ted: This is a general issue with me. I am slow to claim my rights and then I wind up not getting them.
AFB: If you know this then why did you pick Barbara for a relationship?
Ted: She has many positives, the kind that men like.

AFB: So do many other women who aren't nearly as pushy about their feelings getting their way.
Ted: So?
AFB: The likely issue is that you chose her because you weren't ready to assert your emotional rights in a relation.
Ted: How does that help me?
AFB: It tells you where you want to do some work on expanding your personality.
Ted: Is this about assertiveness training?
AFB: It's about having a sense of entitlement to express what you feel when you are with a woman, or with anyone. When you begin to feel that you want to do this, then look for a woman who is more open to how you feel about things.
Ted: I know how to go to work on the first part. But how do I look for the right kind of woman?
AFB: Once you feel like expressing yourself more with a woman, and people in general, you will be likely to attract a woman who feels good about the new you.
Ted: So you're offering hope of things working out better by themselves once I go to work on staking my claim emotionally.
AFB: That's well put and things are likely to happen just the way you say.

Chapter 10.

Irresistible Men

You do something to me,
Something that simply mystifies me.

...from You Do Something to Me
by Cole Albert Porter

There are men who seem to have an irresistible power to attract women. They appear to have an invisible and overwhelming something about themselves that compels women to long for their company. Just a few moments of contact with such men fills women with romantic wishes, provoked by the flood of good feelings that such men create. The irresistible man seems to leave women, and the most beautiful ones too, no choice but to throw their affections at him. Such men form a small part of the male population, yet it is easy to find examples of them almost anywhere. Some are in the public eye, such as political leaders, actors and athletes. However, the great majority of men with this power over women lead otherwise ordinary lives and are known only in their own circles.

Women are drawn to men of the first kind, those in the public eye, because they strike women as being so like the ideals that most women cherish. Women feel a special and romantic thrill when they find men who seem to realize their ideals. A woman increases such a man's irresistible power still more with her unconscious belief that the ideal man can only treat her the way she wants to be treated. A political leader openly promises the ideal of a better life and a better world to everyone, male and female. This stirs images of trust in a woman that make her feel safe and well grounded in life, two very basic needs in a female. The politician's high place in life and his promises color her images of him with great admiration and this is one root of his seductive power.

Successful actors play to the fulfillment of wishes that go frustrated in most people most of the time. Among these wishes is the female need to see parts of the ideal male come to life, and what better place than on stage. One such wish is the longing for the wholesome male who has eyes only for her and who is also sexy in a becoming way. He enchants her with portrayals of loving attention that make her feel wanted and dignified at the same time. Actors bring to life men who will seek her out above all others for the romance that she hopes for but usually finds only in her imagination. The actors that women find irresistible are very good at portraying giving their rapt attention to her and her alone. The man who can place her at center stage is close to her ideal. Women of all ages have cited Robert Redford as an actor who portrays this well and, in their opinions, in real life too! The same is true of Clark Gable though he is of a different era. There are many, many more that can come to mind for you to study.

　The athlete goes directly to the female need to feel overawed by male power, yet with faith that his strength is put to good purpose. The athlete stirs a deep sexual wish because the psyche, male or female, cannot see sex without also seeing power and vice versa. The athlete must play fairly or he will compromise his power to draw women to himself so easily; a woman's fear of abuse of power is never far from her breathless enchantment with male strength. Most women have a deep longing to be swept away by a male's power even though they are not inclined to talk about it. The idea of his power carrying her away sexually presupposes a trust in men that she wishes to discuss even less, especially with men. The male athlete or champion shows immense power from afar, and her spectator role makes her fantasies about him safe. As for close up and alone with him, the public adulation he enjoys will make her want to trust him, at least in the beginning.

　Women cannot help being drawn to men like this — political leaders, actors and athletes — who charm by their positions of power or acclaim in the world. Women are ready to find their greatest ideals in such men and are therefore half won before even meeting one of them. This may sound like an impossible thing to begin to emulate or rival, but there is good news lurking behind this. The good news is that there are reasons to neither envy such men nor to seek to be like them.

　The basis for a woman's interest in them is short lived. Women usually want no more than a passing tryst with such figures, for they easily sense that they are being charmed by a spell that will pass. Once she has sampled the man who intoxicates her, in reality or in her imagination, she quickly returns to her senses and resumes her usual way. A woman's dominant psychology with its longing to be discovered, to trust and to find emotional support in the man she cares for, soon pulls her back to her stable inner longings and wishes. These needs form her basic self and she chooses a lover with them in mind.

A woman knows only too well that if she sampled this kind of man long enough then his power over her would fade and he would soon become no more than an ordinary rival to any other man. She does not want the spell to go away but to live on as a cherished memory. This is probably why most women who become crazed with handsome singers and actors will settle happily for just a few intimate minutes with them. Some want no more than to get within close range of such men or even a simple token such as a handkerchief or glove that he wore.

Irresistible men who are not in the public eye form the second and larger group. It is of greater value and interest than the first group for finding success knowledge. It consists of ordinary men whose irresistible powers come not from their position in the world but from what they do. The ways of such men can be studied, understood and then emulated in your life. Casual thought can make these men look like they form a diverse group but, as you will see, they all share a common something that you too can acquire.

Some men seem to be irresistible because of a basic animal magnetism. A woman who senses this in a man, as well as a sound interest in her from the outset, will be drawn to him. She will see an exciting power in his earthy way and she will find his primal energy close to the way she experiences herself emotionally. She will find it natural to desire him and feel that he is rich in promise. Not all men who have power over women have animal magnetism and it therefore cannot be what makes men irresistible, in general.

Some men sense what key emotions are so, so important to women. This is an intuitive kind of perception in men that is followed by their giving women the very feelings and kind of attention they so much want. These men know how to make an appeal to women's deep inner needs. Their very way makes women feel emotionally understood and satisfies a wish for something from a man that most women cannot get enough of. Not all men who have power over women have this kind intuitive perception and the ability to deliver on it. Like animal magnetism, it therefore cannot be at the heart of what makes men irresistible.

The key difference between doing well and doing very well is found in the idea of authenticity. It is more than honesty or sincerity. The first part of authenticity was given earlier as the discovery principle, meaning that women need to see that you feel you have found great beauty, goodness and promise in her, especially in her ways over her lines. Becoming irresistible carries this to a next level of expression that is richer, freer and more natural. The fellow with animal magnetism is able to express more of what all men have. What he offers is no more than an authentic, that is a richer and more open, expression of what all other men have. Women can only be charmed by such offerings for they reveal a man to her in a way that is much like her own. This means that women see things more easily when they are delivered as easy and welcome self expressions. This is their own way and they can only be charmed to find some of it in you, especially because of their endless curiosity about what it really feels like to be a man. A woman also sees her own way in men who can sense, more easily than most, what emotions are important to her and who can also follow up with expressions that fulfill her emotional wishes.

Women long to see what is real in you because they take all you offer them to be your response to themselves. They are eager to see your interest in them and, finding that, to see just what you are made of. They do not seek an athlete or a hero but simply what it is that makes you a male, and therefore right for them. Their appetite for expressions of how you feel about them and what they do to you is made greater by their awareness that emotional and deeper expressions come less easily to men than women. When a man delivers the goods, so to speak, a woman finds herself charmed by the "man who can," meaning that this man can express what she wants to see and feel. When your interaction with her goes this way, she feels more secure about giving herself to you and feels confident that you are more fitting than others for the gift of herself. The basis for her confidence is seeing you express yourself in a way that she first sees in herself. That way, again, is an open and self-accepting expression of the natural emotions that she stirs in you. Such a way is healthy in both genders but it is found more richly in females, most of the time.

Authenticity appeals to both genders. Something in human nature recognizes a true expression from within and likes the way it feels. When a man expresses himself in this rich and spontaneous way, a woman takes it as a sign that he is trustworthy. She does so because the action reveals some of what the man is and also because women understand such things more easily than men. The same event seen by other men is likely to create feelings of admiration for his being genuine and open. Women also have these feelings but the way of their gender enables them to see more of what the man's expressions are saying.

Authenticity and self esteem go together. A male who feels good about himself is more apt to accept the risk of openness that goes with being authentic. It is not possible to have the free and accepting way with your self that authenticity wants unless you first see how good you are. The male who is authentic has a high enough regard for what he is to want the world to see it, and to be proud of it himself. Women are eager to find men who feel good about themselves this way and they take authenticity as its surest and most natural sign. Women's intuition on this is especially sound, and therefore the more you see and feel your own worth, the easier your successes will become. This will happen because your joy with your own powers will make you feel like letting them show, without any forethought, and this is precisely the spontaneity that women hope to find in men.

An eager young man, call him Eric, found a connecting link between authenticity and charm that can help other men.

Eric: It really does seem that some men can get any woman they want. I wish I knew their secret. (pause) Maybe it's not a secret, but a gift they are born with.

AFB: How about it being a skill?

Eric: You're just telling me what I want to hear.

AFB: Any man can learn to attract women as much as he wants to. It's a question of motivation.

Eric: So you want me to believe there is a right way?

AFB: If I said there's a way to emotional health, would you agree with me?

Eric: Sure, but I don't see the point when it comes to women.

AFB: Emotional health comes when a person learns to let himself be. You connect with women by letting your first reactions to them go to them on their own.

Eric: That's it?

AFB: It's easier said than done but, yes, that's what works. It's about being authentic and it's a form of emotional health.

Eric: There's something missing here. When those irresistible guys get their way there are smiles and excitement everywhere. How does that fit in?

AFB: The men's smiles are genuine expressions of interest in the women. The women take that interest as coming from what the men see in them and that excites them because it is just what they hope for.

Eric: But it seems like these men have a something other men don't and it makes women want to be with them.

AFB: I think you are trying to say that such men are charming, yes?

Eric: Right, and I don't see how that relates to authenticity.

AFB: Charm is basically a man's expression of warm and affectionate interest in a woman, given with respect and dignity. The charm comes from how rich,

and even more, from how natural or unrehearsed the expression is.
Eric: So if I open up more and let women see how they get to me, then I will succeed more because they want to see what they do to me. And the authentic part is about how much of this comes naturally, right?
AFB: This is not something that can be forced. You need to learn to let women see what they do to you. The more you let those emotions do their own thing, the more authentic you are. Women know it when they see it. They take your ability to express your feelings as a sign of high self esteem, and that's another thing that draws them on.
Eric: And the charm part happens by itself as I let my self do its thing without getting in my own way. Is that it?
AFB: That's about it. Charm comes by itself when you become authentic enough.

Eric saw that charm, sexual or otherwise, cannot be artificial even though it can be acquired by learning the art of free and unrehearsed self expression, the giveaway sign of authenticity. Eric worked his way to seeing that most of charm is just letting one's feelings for a female go out on their own toward her. That is why charm and authenticity go hand in hand. Again, the same is true of self esteem and authenticity because the better you feel about yourself, the more easily you will give your expressions to women, including the important ones that they create in the first place.

Most of the grace that people associate with charm is not from practiced motions but from being at ease with your own emotional makeup and letting it go where it wants to go. This is a large part of how to live happily and successfully, and not just with women.

I worked with a female, call her Ellen, who brought up the issue most people assume, that charm is related to grace.

Ellen: There are men that I really can't say no to. They key into just what I want to feel and hear.
AFB: So why is this a problem?
Ellen: Well, they are a joy to be with but I don't like the amount of power they have over me. They are so smooth and seem to know what I want before they even meet me.
AFB: You make them sound like they have some secret knowledge or power. Is that right?
Ellen: That's how it feels.
AFB: How about some examples of men you find charming? Try some popular figures that I will recognize.
Ellen: You mean like actors?
AFB: That's a good place to start.
Ellen: Well, from the old timers, there's Clark Gable. He was so sexy and smooth. And then there was Errol Flynn, he was just a beautiful man and so adorably charming. Later on there are stronger men like Sean Connery. How can a woman say no to men like that? They have a way that circles around a woman so easily and makes her see nothing but him.
AFB: You seem to think that charming men have a finesse or grace to them, is that right?
Ellen: They all do.
AFB: How do you feel about Arnold Schwarzenegger?
Ellen: He's so cute!

AFB: Do you find him charming too?
Ellen: You have to ask?
AFB: Do you find him graceful too?
Ellen: (pause) Well, he is charming. But I wouldn't call him graceful or not graceful. The idea isn't there with him.
AFB: So what makes him charming?
Ellen: Oh, you know! He has such a boyish smile and he gives that big powerful body with such individual attention to everyone he talks to. Maybe it's a European thing. (pause) No, I don't think so.
AFB: So what was charming about Clark Gable, Errol Flynn and Sean Connery?
Ellen: I need some time with this. (pause) Well, when I think of myself with them I see them giving me that same sweet attention and interest in me as Arnold.

When a woman says that she finds a man charming she has a number of things in mind. The most obvious is that he is getting to her. Ellen's narrative reveals that the key way he gets to her is with a delighted interest in her. Incidentally, Ellen's issue was how her narcissism could not resist the attention of men, making it easy to see that upbeat male attention for the female is one powerful part of how men charm women.

The charming man sees a woman as sexy in a wholesome way. He welcomes her emotional color and wants to enjoy getting to know her inner ways because those magical, inner ways do more to make her sexy than her lines. Charm also makes a woman feel honored by making a statement about her dignity and worth. This is one reason why, in the age of monarchs, a charming manner was so fitting, even demanded, at court. Everything about charm comes less from what is said than its delivery. That is why a kiss on the hand, given with true feeling for the lady, goes so far. It tells a woman that not only is she sexy and beautiful but she is also to be revered as a person. Try it and see. You may feel that it has passed out of style, like a bow, but she will glow over such a gesture and bubble into your life.

You can develop charm. At bottom, it is an advanced form of authenticity where your first feelings come out to her under their own power and with no obstacle in their way. Your progress in being genuine will also bring you higher levels of personal fulfillment and increase your success in general, not just with women. There are many ways to acquire more authenticity or charm. For one, take a bigger bite out of life and the world by learning to enjoy more activities and finding more interests. These things will invite your feelings out to life and make you more colorful. When idle, pay some attention to what you saw in others, of both genders, and what emotions they stirred in you. This will make it easier for you to express the wishes that women create in you and to win their longing for you with tasty samples of your emotional energy, a thing they simply cannot get enough of.

Make another kind of plunge into life, a more passionate one, to get to higher levels of charm. This calls for a mix of activity, study and imitation. You will find the raw material by watching videos or movies where it is well portrayed. There are many fine pieces of literature and poetry, written to enchant on the basis of a charming male, that are worth your attention. You can also watch life around you closely, ready to see and then study men who are charming. If you are more serious than most about it, you can take lessons in dancing and other art forms or spend time in the company of actors and performers. The last are people who will show you a short cut to what personal expression really means, for their livelihood depends on doing it correctly.

You will not need unusual authenticity to be adept with charm and to create more of the success you want. Nature wants success to come to you with the easy flow of life, for otherwise nature works against itself. Again, it comes most easily when you learn to simply let your expressions go out as a first response to what stirred them to begin with. The more you let your inner self run free before the woman who beguiles you, the more irresistible she will find you. The more you express your real interest in her, the more charming she will find you. Do both of these things and you are very likely to succeed most of the time, if not always.

GUIDED EXERCISE. Recall a time when you found someone authentic or charming. Follow what your images do to your emotions and what your emotions would do to a woman.

GUIDED ANSWER. "There's a man I see a lot at singles' events. He's around 30, not bad looking and a bit overweight. I watch him because women do not find him attractive at first. But then he goes over to them and things change. He gives them a big smile and shows much interest in them, and then everything changes. The women turn to him, give him smiles and are eager to talk with him. He only spends a few minutes talking then chooses one of them to dance with and she goes so, so willingly. When he dances with her he is still giving her this smile of confident interest in her and it's amazing how the woman responds to it.

"This makes me feel like I do most but not all of what he does. He shows an interest in women with a smile and so do I. But he comes more from an excited interest in them than I do. It's like he makes the woman feel how happy he is to have found her. His feelings go out to her more easily than mine. I know that I feel what he feels when he sees a woman, but he is much better at making it show. He is a charmer and I have to guess that the charm is not in his looks, his porky build and his ungainly movements. It has to be in how easily his good feelings go from him to her.

"It seems that a woman really wants to see that she can make a man feel that way. His presentation is all about how good he feels finding her and watching her open up more of herself to him. If I presented myself like that to a woman, she would probably respond the same way. He succeeds so much because he lets his real feelings show and because the interest and attention he gives women are real. All I have to do is unplug myself a little more and then I can do that too. If women find his easy and adoring attention so irresistible, when he isn't even all that attractive, then I should do at least as well."

Chapter 11.

The Darker Side of Women

Heaven has no rage like love to hatred turned,
Nor hell a fury like a woman scorned.

...from The Mourning Bride by William Congreve

The female of the species is more deadly than the male.

...from The Female of the Species by Rudyard Kipling

You may be wondering why this chapter is introduced with two quotations while most of the others have only one. It is to emphasize the power of the dark side of women's nature. Prior chapters have emphasized how nature gifts women with certain intuitions and a remarkable beauty, both distinctive of their gender. Their need to trust in matters of love and romance, and to give themselves to the happiness and support of others has also been emphasized. The theme of their generosity in love has been there, more between the lines than spelled out. The depth and scope of these wonderful qualities of the female suggest the formidable rage that can overtake her when she feels she has given in vain, or worse, has been deceived. The female's yen to generously give her beauty and joyful ways to the male she cares for makes her vulnerable to not getting the return she hopes for from the outset. When she is let down her sense of injury runs deep and a furious, often vengeful, anger quickly replaces the tenderness she once felt.

Women invest themselves in relations more fervently than men. Their make up is more monogamous because both their biology and their part in human history have made it so. Almost every female longs for a man to whom she will give as much loving goodness as he wants, provided that he will be hers alone. A woman as one who would send so much goodness to a man becomes one who would send so much wrath to the man who trifles with her offer. It will probably surprise most men to hear that a woman's need to be seen as sexy or seductive has little to with her anger when it comes. Their most important inner wishes and needs come from their need to give life through love and to be seen as one who does so. Women expect men to support this part of them and when they decide that a man is trustworthy it is mostly because they feel that he will do so. A woman also expects the man who enjoys her love to see its life giving power to his personality and to their world as lovers. When women say that they want men to see them as special, this is at the center of what they mean.

A woman who was articulate and in good contact with her emotions spelled out the issues quite clearly. Call her Michelle.

Michelle: It's not comfortable being this angry even though I feel I have a right to be. (pause) Jimmy was

very good to me and I just assumed he wanted things to go the same way I did. I had a relation in mind, not just play. It felt right and natural to be good to him when he was so good to me.
AFB: You feel deceived?
Michelle: I feel undone. I feel thwarted. I feel like a fool. (pause) Before we met I was looking for someone to care about and get close to, someone to give myself to and have the good life with. Jimmy gave me that strong and bubbly interest that I had to respond to. I just assumed he wanted it to go somewhere. Oh I enjoyed the play time of getting to know each other, but I saw that as the opening act, not the finish.
AFB: So the relationship came to a fork in the road, you wanted to go one way and he another. Is that it?
Michelle: Sort of, but it's not that innocent.
AFB: Why not?
Michelle: I could deal with this with much less anger if I felt he did not know where I wanted things to go. I could say so he wanted play and I wanted love and I only saw the difference later. But I'm sure that he saw all along what I wanted. I'm sure he saw my hope that he would love me and be with me.
AFB: So he made a bad bargain for your affection?
Michelle: That's how it feels. He knew what I was looking for and he knew his wishes were somewhere else. I suppose things like this happen all the time, but that's no consolation.
AFB: And the hard part is...?
Michelle: The blow to my sincerity and my pride is the worst of it. I feel like I misinvested myself, taking a risk because I trusted where things would go.
AFB: Any chance that Jimmy felt you were only out for fun like him?
Michelle: I don't think so! This is not a hard thing to see. You know, women are good at picking up on these

things, if not at first then eventually like me. He played me and I saw what I wanted to see until the frustration got to me.

Deceit and deception are among the least favored words in a woman's vocabulary. They are words that women associate with the emotion of humiliation, and that emotion is more painful for most of them than for men. If a woman comes to realize that a man has manipulated her for sexual pleasure her major resentment will not be over being exploited but over being humiliated and deceived. There is such a thing as female pride and male insincerity will flush it out. Where men don't like to feel weak or ineffective, women do not want to feel that their dignity has been compromised. Most women deal with weakness and vulnerability better than the average male and most men deal with injured pride and letdown better than the average female.

There are things more hurtful to a woman than being humiliated. They are found among the forces that work against how she sees the meaning of her nature. Men who devote their powers to thwarting a woman's purpose are flirting with a greater and darker fury than they are likely to imagine. At the heart of her purpose are creative love supported by her intuition and a strong sense of commitment. Women find great fulfillment and satisfaction in what their beauty and ways can do for the man they love. They take great pride in their powers and most enjoy a deep sense of security with how seductive those powers are. This position is so deep in women that most would rather not be than lose their creative purpose and its beauty. The peak moments in a woman's life are where she sees her seductive power over men or where she sees how much joy and happiness her ways bring to the man she loves. That is, more of her joy and fulfillment comes from seeing her effect on men than from what men do to her.

Michelle's Jimmy was concerned about the outcome with her. He was in touch with his feelings, like Michelle, but not their meanings.

Jimmy: I don't like the ways things turned out with Michelle. I never meant to hurt her. I don't understand why she is taking it so hard.
AFB: What did you want with her?
Jimmy: Well, the pleasure of her company. She's good looking, sensitive, affectionate and loves life. When I first saw her I thought she'd be fun to get to know and be with. And she was! We had very good times together for the first few months. We visited far away places and had them all to ourselves. I looked forward to being with her. (pause) Then after a few months she began to lose enthusiasm for me. We talked about it but it didn't go anywhere.
AFB: Did she tell you what was on her mind?
Jimmy: Not really. I mean she would talk in a round about way but I never left the conversation seeing a problem to work on.
AFB: Did you tell her what you wanted with her?
Jimmy: Sure.
AFB: And...?
Jimmy: And what?
AFB: Was she content with your goals? Did she add anything?

Jimmy: She never seemed to have a problem with how much I enjoyed her. Or how much fun we had together. (pause) Did she add anything? Let me see. Well, she made it clear that she wasn't satisfied with where things were going. So I asked her where she wanted them to go. I never got a straight answer.
AFB: She wanted you to sense what was important to her about her feelings for you. She wanted you to know where she wanted her feelings to go.
Jimmy: What does that mean?
AFB: She enjoyed you too. She let her feelings grow and deepen but with hope that the relation would go from fun to something deeper. She wanted you.
Jimmy: But that's not where I was coming from!
AFB: She felt she was giving herself in vain.
Jimmy: Yeah, I get that. But why end a relation on that basis?
AFB: You were both enjoying yourselves and that was enough for you. It was not enough for her.
Jimmy: But why is she so angry?
AFB: She feels that she gave a great deal of herself. She finds her emotions all wrapped around you with no hope of getting what they want.
Jimmy: I didn't mean to hurt her and I don't want her anger.
AFB: Don't hold your breath. This is the kind of thing that women don't soon forget, if ever.
Jimmy: So does this mean I have to declare my intentions with every next romance?
AFB: It would probably be a good idea to be on the lookout for what the next one wants. Why start something that is going to end this way?
Jimmy: Maybe I could change my goals.
AFB: That happens when it happens. For now it's probably a good idea to choose females who are out

to enjoy life, like yourself. When you feel differently about what you want, then think about what next to do.

A woman wants a man to use his power to work with her, even when she has no more than fun in mind for a relationship. Working with her includes considering what is important to her as important to both of you. This means sharing what she likes where that feels natural and otherwise supporting her likes. Working with her also includes the obvious lending a hand where you are stronger or more adept than she is. It includes telling her how to get closer to you, to be there for you and showing her how to share your ups and downs, and so on.

Her heart is set on making the man who works with her into a uniquely important love object for her emotions and her creative ways. She sees this as a gift of both love and gratitude that works toward the fulfillment of the man she cares about, as well as herself. She will want you to join her emotions and the plans that she has for them in doing this. She wants to live with quiet trust in you, knowing all the while that her fondest wish is to give you herself and her very special ways. Her largest meaning of trust is that you will be there for her and that your avid interest in her will go on and on. Her trust means that she first needs to be confident that your male powers join her female purposes and work willingly with her. A woman's tendency to be possessive can be an expression of this, but her wish to give herself because she first trusts you, and then loves you, remains the main issue.

The up side of a woman's dark side is that the strength of her wrath reveals how very much she has to give and how very much she wants to give. Most men are not likely to ever encounter the dark energy described here. Most men sense and respect how important a woman's regard for her place in love is to her and in doing so most men safeguard themselves. The more you make what is so important to her equally important to you, the greater her reward of love and affection. Women can be extraordinarily generous with their love, and there is no practical limit to how much they will give if they are first confident that you share their sense of what love is and can be. The finest safeguard against her dark side is your wish to grow a genuine affection with her that respects each of you. She will instinctively and happily respect, admire and reward such intentions in you.

The Darker Side of Women 129

GUIDED EXERCISE. Go to a time when you could see what a woman wanted in love or romance. Imagine what her experience is like, first with getting her wish, and then with not getting it.

GUIDED ANSWER. Here is the gist of how this exercise went for a man, call him Hal, the first time he did it.

Hal: I feel like I'm turning a corner in my current relation. For almost a year we have had fun and romance together. But it was always open ended, at least for me. Then she started to change or maybe I just began to notice what she was about all along.
AFB: What did that do to you?
Hal: I began to feel that maybe there is a next step after fun and romance. It became hard to picture life without her. The more I wanted to be with her, the more I wondered what she was feeling and what was important to her. I began to wonder if maybe she wanted to go to a next level before me. Maybe she got there first and was patiently waiting for me to catch up.
AFB: Did you wonder what might become of the two of you, one way or the other?
Hal: Yes, I did. First I thought of how I felt for her and how life might be if she felt the same way. This made me realize that she was hoping for the same thing I was, but probably before me. At first I just wanted what I wanted, for us to be lovers. Then I began to get anxious and didn't know why. (pause) Eventually I realized how strong her wishes were and that I was anxious because of what might happen if I let her down. I didn't like the way that felt but my good feelings for her kept returning and that made

me hope for the happiness we both wanted with each other. I could see how giving and warm and sweet she would be if she were sure that we were each other's.
AFB: What happens if she doesn't get her wish.
Hal: Well, her wish is the same as mine and that's not something I really want to think about.
AFB: Try it anyway.
Hal: That anxious feeling is back. She is hurt and resentful.
AFB: What is this like for her?
Hal: She feels hurt, let down, mislead, frustrated. She's angry because she feels cheated. She was about to make me her life and her world.
AFB: As far as she's concerned there is no greater offering she could make.
Hal: I get that. And I also want what she wants, so I am not going to worry about it.

PART II
GOING FOR GOLD

There is much more skill and knowledge in your future after you have mastered the basics. The important basics are about the near identity of men and women in most areas, the immense importance to a woman of feeling that you have discovered her, her need to feel supported by you and to find you trustworthy and her deep wish to be the emotional heart and energy of your relationship with her. This knowledge forms a good foundation for a deeper understanding of what women want and for the skills that create your success.

The first chapter of PART II answers the question as to why women are so taken with the figure of the knight. This opens the issues of male power, female trust, and her longing for support from and to be centered by the male in her life. Material on your options in relationships, the nature of male power and how to use it for success with ambivalent women follows. Avoidable women, advanced ways of flirting and the healthy power of sexual attraction round out this part.

The material in PART II will give you a deeper and more immediate awareness of what success wants as well as how to achieve it with less effort and more joy. Your harvest should include, in addition to more success and enjoyment, more poise in your delivery and a delightful confidence in your outcomes.

Chapter 12.

The Lure of the Knight

There looms, large, uncertain, dim but glittering, the legend of King Arthur and the Knights of the Round Table...It is all true, or it ought to be; and more and better besides.

...from The Birth of Britain by Winston S. Churchill

The age of chivalry will never die because it will always live in the hearts of women. The very idea of chivalry feeds the pride they take in their beauty and the way they feel their dignity to be rooted in the finest of life and nature itself. And you had better notice it! In their souls is the hope of an ideal man to whom they long to give everything. What they see in their ideal and the hopes they set by it are found in the figure of the knight.

There are many keys to the female heart and perhaps the best among them is trust. Women are enchanting creatures of immense pride and they will not risk injured pride lightly. They will play with you but keep you waiting until they feel that you merit their trust. And who is more trustworthy than the one who will take chances and flirt with danger for her sake? They have taken to their hearts the idea that discretion is the better part of valor, and how they long to reward the man who is valorous for them.

Much is to be gained by taking seriously just how much women are taken with the romantic ideal of the knight and what he means to them. In fact, this ideal is found in women from cultures that do not even have a concept of knighthood or a well formed tradition of it. The image has a deep root in their wish to be sure that the male's superior strength will serve them and make them want to offer him their grateful rewards. A female also sees the rewards she so willingly gives her knightly male as the way to grow love from him to her.

There is good reason for women to admire the door-holding man or the fellow who offers to help her with her packages. Inwardly, a woman sees such a man as continuous with an earlier time where similar acts meant that he wanted to be her champion. The gleam of admiration flashing in her eyes when you offer her assistance is saying that she accepts you as protector of her person and her worth. It also means that she plans to reward you for your exertions! To her, you are valorous when you use your strength to support what is important to her and put it between her and harm's way. This lifts her spirit with greater hopes for what she values and gives her a welcome assurance that you wish to work for well with her.

She feels the thrill of the knight's image come alive when you work with her on the things that she finds important, and this reaches much more than her safety. She especially feels this way about your strength and support with things she cannot achieve by herself, or only with difficulty. When you stir the knight's image in her she feels a world of new possibility opening to her and her warmest, most affectionate thoughts turn quickly to you. One part of her ideal man is a knight whose way will lift her from her concerns and carry her off to the love of her fondest dreams. You do this whenever she sees that you are happy to work with her and be there for her.

Courtesy to a woman is kin to assisting her and carries a similar meaning. It tells her that you have a high regard for her and esteem her as a person, and she takes this to mean that you will act to uphold the dignity and worth that you see in her. Women unconsciously see courtesy in a man as a thing that the charms of their psyche have created. They treasure how this as their handiwork makes them feel because they regard every good coming from you to them as first created by what you find in them. This is, of course, a point already made several times, but worth repeating. Women also find in courtesy a royal message to others about how she wants to be treated, and she proudly displays the fellow who does so for all to see. A woman finds the same or similar meanings when you dance with her for there you have the lead and she relies on you in public, just the like damsel and the knight errant. Dancing of the close up kind gives her the thrill of feeling for herself how much stronger and directed you are than she, and this can make her feel helpless in the happiest way.

The romantic meaning of the knight in the West is part of the story of Camelot. The most numerous, if not the most familiar, Camelot image is that of the knight who champions a lady and who announces this by fastening a small outer garment of hers to some part of his armor or person. The knight usually defends the lady in trial by combat, meaning that the claims of the just or truthful party will be proven by the victory of the knight who defends them. The implicit meaning is that her beauty inspires him to fight to win and that he sees great merit in her. The unspoken meaning on the male side has much to do with sexual gain. The unspoken meaning from the female side is also seductive, but it goes much further.

In the legend, King Arthur founded Camelot for many reasons, all of them coming together under the role of justice and valor in an ideal society. Defending a worthy cause against great odds, protecting the weak and the helpless innocent, and other like themes are all part of the Camelot ideal. That is the ideal that grows quickly and eagerly in the female heart, from youth onward. Her meaning of the knight is tied to upholding what is right, good and decent, especially against odds and with personal risk, or at least inconvenience. Her ideal respects the fact that a female really is not as strong as the average male and, what's more, that the female is more prone to becoming lost to overly rich emotions than the average male. The male enters as a rescuing knight who remedies both of these things by his certain presence and his fondness for taking action.

It is natural to feel that the one who would defend you and uphold you against others will never hurt you. The acts of courtesy and respect that you give a woman build a sense of trust in her that you will always work with her and be good to her. It is not merely fear of rejection, or the loathsome prospect of abuse, that speaks from the back of their minds, but the greater fear of humiliation and injured pride. The better you are to them, the more they feel satisfied that they have awakened and nurtured the goodness within you. Today's women are true to the damsels of Camelot on this point, for like them, today's women feel that the good a man does for them comes from what he found in them and that he wishes to tell the world about it.

A perky young woman, call her Dale, was so delighted over meeting her knight that she was concerned over how to keep him. Her narrative reveals much of the knight from the female side.

Dale: I met the most wonderful fellow the other night. I felt such assurance from him that he would be there for me even though we only just met. Yes, he made me feel pretty, but a lot of men do that. But he also made me feel like what I value can be important to him. It's not easy to meet a man who makes you feel that way!
AFB: All this is good news. So what's the issue?
Dale: Well, he really made an impression. And, you know, I want to make sure it goes right with him.
AFB: You're quite attractive and in a number of ways. So why are you concerned?
Dale: Because I don't often meet a man like this.
AFB: You strike me as having good judgment. I don't see cause for concern.
Dale: You're not getting it! I'm ready to give the store away to get this one!
AFB: Oh, I see, you're afraid you'll be swept away and do something rash.

Dale: Uh huh. Too bad you're not a woman. Then you would know what it feels like to be with a man that you feel you really can trust if he would only become interested in you.
AFB: So you feel he would go the distance for you, maybe even put himself before you, yes?
Dale: He's strong and romantic too. He makes light of things that concern me and unsettle me. I feel I can give everything to him, including my cares, because it feels like he wants to care.
AFB: Sounds like you picked a winner.
Dale: I told you! And I want to keep him before another gal swoops him up. (pause) What should I do?
AFB: Well, after you calm down, I would remind myself that every knight wants his reward. But don't make it too easy for him.
Dale: That means I will have to put my head before my heart. But I'll do it, at least for a while!

Every woman has to deal with how vulnerable she feels when she commits herself to a lasting relation. However independent and self sufficient she may become financially, her dependency on the man's reliability will continue to concern her and cause some anxiety. The female image of the knight has come to represent the man who would be ideal in light of her apprehensions. The more she trusts that you honor her person and her purpose, the more she will give herself to you. In legend and in actual history the knight originated as a person whose presence assured protection and dispelled anxiety or fear. The current romantic image of the knight still does that. A difference, between then and now, is that the original concern was with mortal danger and the present concern is with your availability, sustaining presence and esteem for what she values.

The figure of the knight also portrays remarkably well how male energy can drive women crazy. Women see him as romantic, dashing, sexy and gallant. It takes her breath away to see in him her ideals on the best and fairest use of superior male strength with commitment to a high purpose. She colors the ideal with her romantic hopes and sees the knight's valor as serving love, goodness and security in her life. She also sees in that image the traits that promise her that she can trust the man who is getting to her. A woman's regard for the knight, like men's, begins with his strength and power. When a woman meets you and is taken with you, she also hopes to find ways and sentiments that are like the knight's. This means that she has a need to feel that she creates in you the wish to give your strength and power to worthwhile ends, especially with her.

The knight is a romantic and inspiring symbol for both sexes. His image and lore tell the male a great deal on how to get the good things in life — with more than just with women. The message is not in the archaic figure of the warrior, whose destructive imagery turns women off, but in the knight's devotion to upholding decency, not just women's but everyone's. In the Camelot legend, every knight had his lady, and most had loves as spectacular as their heroic roles in legend. However the legend was born, its tale of gallantry grew rich in images of beautiful women swooning with love for the knight's promise to love them and uphold fair play for their sake. The legend was inspired by an actual King Arthur who defeated

Roman forces in his native England. It was romanticized as it then moved between England and France. Yet for all that, women all over the world long to find the images of Camelot in their love life.

GUIDED EXERCISE. Recall a time when you were a lady's knight. Study the good feelings that she offers you in reply to your being there for her.

GUIDED ANSWER. Here is how this exercise went with a young man who had an appetite for life. Call him Adam.

Adam: I'm not sure I have ever been a knight to a female.
AFB: You never held a door open for a lady, you never offered to help a lady with her packages or her car and so on?
Adam: Oh yes, I've done those things. (pause) Let me see. There's a gal at work who's really sweet. The other day she was trying to copy some material and was having a hard time of it. I saw my opportunity and offered to help her. She smiled at once and it was obvious that she welcomed the help. I'm sure she knew I was flirting with her.
AFB: Uh huh, that's likely. Try to stay with what your offer of help did to her.
Adam: OK. She looked relieved and grateful at the same time. In the middle of it the machine stopped. She didn't know what to do but I did. It needed toner. I replaced it and that really got to her!
AFB: Why do you think that happened?
Adam: I guess she saw my mechanical skill as more of a male thing and was glad I was there to use it for her.
AFB: Anything else?
Adam: Like what?
AFB: Like how does she want men to treat women.
Adam: Hmmm. Well, I feel that she likes it when a man uses his talent or strength to help. She likes the

idea of men using what they have to be constructive. (pause)
AFB: Keep going.
Adam: Well, she's the sort of female that can make most men want to be with her but most men don't get very far with her. Maybe she doesn't like what she sees in most others.
AFB: Maybe most others are more interested in a quick connection with her rather than what is important to her.
Adam: So my helping her at the copy machine made a statement about my taking what is important to her as important to me? And maybe that made her feel she could count on me?
AFB: Yes, and when a female feels that way she soon comes to trust you as one who deserves her affections.
Adam: I can live with that.

Chapter 13.

Dates, Mates and More

'S wonderful! 'S marvelous —
You should care for me!

...from Funny Face by Ira Gershwin

You will find fresh opportunities with women as you learn to see and understand what they are looking for. You will also find that you have many more options with them. Women are deeply psychological creatures who know the world by how it makes them feel, and they often reveal this with a remarkable oblivion for logic. This kind of awareness of women's nature will increase your social skills by revealing what they seek in you and this, in turn, will make your interactions with them more effective and satisfying. Many of the things that once passed you by as negligible or unimportant will leap into the foreground, telling you to pay attention and showing you how to seize the moment. You will get more of what you want, and this will make it desirable to look more closely at what your growing success skills can bring you. As your confidence grows it becomes prudent, perhaps even necessary, to ask what kind of rewards you wish to enjoy for your efforts.

There are three types of relations you may enjoy with women. You can date in the usual sense of the word, usually seeking no more than fun and pleasure. You can look about, or prospect, for a mate or some version of a deeper and longer term relationship. Or you can be with women for personal growth and prospective purposes, such as learning. These types do not exclude one another and two or all three can be present at the same time.

Dating for fun usually begins in early youth when people are just beginning to experiment with the new and amazing chemistry of puberty. Adolescents have little awareness of how their new feelings relate to the many astonishing body changes they experience at the same time. The fun and exhilaration of dating is also nature's way of showing them how these two — feelings and body parts — go together. This process repeats in subtle ways later in life. One stage where it repeats almost without notice is at the peaking of sexual drive. This usually occurs in the twenties for both genders, with the female somewhat earlier and the male somewhat later. The challenge for both genders is how to rework the way their new body powers best relate to their emotional lives. The peaking of sexual drive in both genders often goes unnoticed. This probably happens because both genders are so involved with learning how to enjoy it.

Dating for fun has a place at every stage of life and most people return to it many times at various points in their life. This can occur for a number of reasons. People who are going through divorce, separation or the end of another kind of long term, committed relation usually feel a need to date. Doing so helps them to work the issues brought up by the end of their last relation and helps keep those issues from contaminating their next relation. The glitter and excitement of dating for fun opens people in this kind of situation to new options in life and helps them to deal with the unwelcome mood that generally follows a loss. Like exercise, dating can clear your energy, lift your mood and make it easier for you to see what recent events mean and how to make a fresh start.

There are other transition points in life where dating can help to expand you. One occurs when you are entering a new stage of life. Most males enter such a transition in the late twenties or early thirties, after the peaking of sexual drive. Nature follows up that peaking with a great flourish of personal powers to support it. These include more assertiveness, a deeper drive to create a sense of self or identity that says "This is whom I am," the need to build a secure place in life and the world, and more. These new powers are strongly interpersonal and it is both a joy and an opportunity to get to know the new powers in the company of some new females, that is, by dating. In fact, it could be argued that nature's intention is for the male learn to master his new powers in the company of females.

An upbeat and sensitive man in his late twenties described his experience at this time of life. Call him Chris. He was trying to find a center of mass in his changing experience.

Chris: I'm almost thirty now and if someone didn't tell me, I would not have noticed my drive increasing. I guess I just got caught up in it. What I do notice is how nature is turning up the volume on a lot of my emotions.

AFB: Like what?

Chris: Well, I feel stronger, more like I want to do things and take a bite out of life. More and more I feel like I can make things happen.

AFB: What parts of life do you have in mind?

Chris: At work, in my love life, in sports and with my friends. I guess it's impacting everywhere. In some ways this is like being a kid again, you know, a teenager.

AFB: Keep going.

Chris: It's like the teens because there's a lot of new stuff coming into view. It's like becoming a little more each day, but it's better.

AFB: Better in what way?

Chris: Well, I may be a little confused by the amount of change in myself now. But when I was a teenager, I didn't have a clue as to what was going on. It took years of groping around and making silly, embarrassing mistakes to begin to understand myself. But now I have a head start on myself. I sorted out that earlier stuff and what happens now is, like I said, mostly turning up the volume.

AFB: The way you describe it I would not think you had any difficulty with it.

Chris: The major issue is where, how and when to best use it.

AFB: Any thoughts on that?

Chris: It seems easier to use the new me at work, with friends and in sports. But it's not so easy with the ladies. I feel awkward and uncertain there. But I have a hunch that my greatest gains can come from working this growth with them.

AFB: Are you thinking of a relationship or dating?

Chris: It's too soon for a relationship. I think sampling the flowers, so to speak, would help a lot. Different women draw out different parts of me. It's a nice experience even though it makes me up tight, even nervous.

AFB: Do you feel that maybe nature is giving you these new powers mostly for the females?

Chris: I need to think that through, but just now I would say that makes sense. I do find that after being with someone new, or finding a new side of a gal I already know, that I am more in touch with myself and that makes me feel more together and more confident.

Prospecting, that is, dating in search of someone with whom to have a deeper relationship, comes after adolescence — usually long after — for most people. Sometimes that more serious relationship evolves from what began as dating with no more than fun in mind; if so, then this is a healthy and happy outcome. The yen to find a soul mate creates a very conscious wish in most men and something of a deliberate search for Miss Right usually follows. At the least, a readiness to recognize "the right one" comes over a man. If your search for a soul mate goes frustrated longer than you feel it should, then it is likely a good idea to take a closer at what you have been doing.

Nature provides such a rich variety of personalities and personal styles in both genders that it is not at all probable for an earnest search to go hungry for very long. This leads to a fork in the road question: is the failure to find a soul mate due to not seeing that many women have been right for you all along, or is it really the case that you would recognize Miss

Right if she were before you but she simply has not crossed your path? One fork leads to accepting that there is still more time to be spent in dating for fun, sampling your options and getting to know what you prefer, favor or need in females. The other fork means that your ship has not yet come in but that you really do want someone for a closer and deeper relationship. This second fork also means that your judgment and sense of women are maturing at a good clip.

If you feel that you want that someone special but are frustrated in your search, how do you know which fork in the road is yours? For one, an earnest search should be able to more easily manage frustration than one that is begun before its time or without enough commitment. If your frustration level becomes uncomfortable, and certainly if it leads to resentment, then it is likely that you need to spend more time dating and sampling the many lovelies all around you. A good sign that now is the time for Miss Right is the inclination to cheerfully apply the energy of mild frustration to a change of strategy. The change could be in where you look for her, the approach you choose to take or even in the kind of female you are looking for. Flexibility goes more with a healthy search grounded in readiness than with a premature search, the latter often giving itself away in the poor way it manages frustration.

Sometimes a return to dating just for fun will put you more in touch with where you are at and resolve the uncertainty. This kind of dating will soon leave you feeling alone, empty and short of your goals if you really do want a deeper tie with a woman. But if it is not yet time, then chances are that dating for fun will feel more natural and comfortable for you. A positive rule of thumb here is that the more gingerly you shake off let downs and resume your search with optimism, the more likely it is that the timing is right. Another good rule of thumb is that the more driven your quest for her is, the less likely it is that the timing is right. The fact is that driven behavior is usually a sign that something else in the personality, very different from what the drive itself seeks, needs more attention. For example, a man driven to date beautiful but frustrating women is likely to be struggling to accept that he deserves much better than he is giving himself.

Dating can have neither fun nor the search for a mate as its primary aim. There are times when its main purpose is personal fulfillment or cultivating some personal strengths. As noted, this is actually one of the main goals of dating in puberty and it often recurs in the various stages of life. I have often heard people joking about having a "meaningless relationship." Their broad smile and pleasant humor made it easy to see that there was in fact a great deal of meaning in the relationship. It was a meaning of a different kind from getting close and seeking long term intimacy with a female. The meaning was mostly in the fun and excitement of finding new parts of the self by enjoying life with an affectionate female in an open ended way. Another meaning was in no more than clearing their energy so as to become open to fresh possibilities, a good idea when coming out of an unhappy or unworkable relationship.

Dating of this kind differs from dating for fun and from dating with a mate in mind in a very specific way. Most men are quite aware of dating for the one reason or the another, that is, fun versus Miss Right. However, when most men date for reasons of personal fulfillment and the discovery of new possibilities, they do not fully realize what they are doing. What's more, they often describe what they are doing as "idle time," "time out," "a meaningless relation," or they mislabel it as dating for fun. Certainly the fun and exhilaration are there, but here the prime goal is not in the good feelings but in how dating is growing a new and larger self.

Another and, in my view, too much neglected variety of a relation with a female is friendship[1]. In my life I have found that women make good friends and that they are often better friends than males in a number of ways. I have generally found them to be more reliable, more eager to help and more supportive than men. Their sensitivity to what things mean emotionally and their willingness to help manage emotions with success has impressed me many times. In fact, it has been a blessing many times over! They have often charmed me and made me laugh with their very private views on the men in their lives — and vice versa.

A friendship with a woman is an excellent opportunity to see close up how she admires men whom she regards as trustworthy and constructive. This is easy to see when she shares with you her wish that a certain kind of male, in view to both of you, will flirt with her. She will be eager to tell you, as her friend, what she sees and, yes, she well knows that she is giving you what she regards as an inside secret. A woman

---

[1] This observation is not based on the research supporting this book. It is the author's personal experience.

will tell you in friendship, and in no uncertain terms, what she savors in men and what she feels she ought to avoid. She will tell you these things for as long as you are a friend and not a romantic prospect. Her view on the man she sees as a romantic prospect is that he is supposed to know these things without being told.

Friendship with a woman is guaranteed protection from hurting her, as long as you do not want to be romantically involved with her. Women manage injuries to friendship with men better than injuries to their heart in love and romance. The sporting side of their nature comes out in friendship with a male. They will gladly share with you most of the things they only share with their lady friends, and much of their laughter will come from watching your eyes open at all the things you never saw that were always there. Friendship with a woman is not a guarantee that she will help you with your relations with other women because her competitive nature overtakes her when it comes to being found desirable. It would take a woman of unusual maturity to help you as your friend in a romantic attachment to another woman, but this does happen too.

GUIDED EXERCISE. Compare your goals in your relations with women with the qualities in women that you favor. Begin by recalling your goals and then recalling what you like in women. How do the two line up?

GUIDED ANSWER. Here is how this exercise went with a spontaneous young man, call him Gary, who tended to succeed without knowing why.

Gary: What do I like in women? Hmmm. Well, beauty is important. So is a perky personality and a love of life.
AFB: Anything else?
Gary: Sure. A good sex drive is important too.
AFB: That's it?
Gary: What else is there?
AFB: We'll get to that later. Now recall a woman whose company you enjoyed more than most.
Gary: Well, there was Allison. She was something else.
AFB: How so?
Gary: She was very attractive and had a saucy way that made you want to talk with her. She was such fun to be with!
AFB: What kinds of things did you like to do together?
Gary: We loved to hike in the woods and admire nature. That made us feel close. We would often fall into deep conversations. We also liked shows and museums. Allison could really get lost in what a painting did to her. Then we would talk about it for hours afterwards.
AFB: Now back track. You said you that beauty in women is important, a perky personality, a love of life and a good sex drive. Allison scores high on the first three, perhaps on the fourth...

Gary: She was a good lover!
AFB: That's good. But your description of what you enjoyed most in Allison was her depth and substance.
Gary: So what?
AFB: If depth and substance is as or more important than what you described then maybe it would be a good idea to look for women who have more of those qualities. Maybe even put depth and substance at the top of your wish list.
Gary: I don't like women who are heady. They can be out of touch with the common sense things that are fun. I like women who really appreciate life and ideas. I wonder why I left that out?
AFB: Probably because its importance to you makes you take it for granted. That can run the risk of missing it when it's in front of you.
Gary: That happened already. I pay more attention to good looks and nice lines than anything else, at least at first. That's made me lose my option with the kind of gal I really wanted a few times.

Chapter 14.

The Immortal Male

What a piece of work is man!
How noble in reason!
how infinite in faculty!
in form, in moving, how express and admirable!
in action how like an angel!
in apprehension how like a god!

...from Hamlet by William Shakespeare

Men drive women just as crazy they do men. Women are just cooler about it. Being the proud creatures they are makes them unwilling to say it is so, but it is. The prospect of finding a male who will complete and well order their inner experience never ceases to make them glow with hope and happy expectation. They admire the way a male can direct his strength with focus and deliberation. They salute and send their hearts to the male capacity to clear obstacles in the path of success. In their eyes the power of the male way is as timeless and enduring as their beauty is to males.

It is more for the male, than the female, to take chances and even to live dangerously on the path to achieving his goals. This is a male way that women look upon with envy, wishing they had more of it for themselves. They are given to taking more secure paths than men to their goals. When women are willing to take chances it is usually less than the risk a male would accept under the same circumstances. When they say that men make them feel secure one of their truest meanings is that men lighten their anxious concern over dealing with risk and uncertainty. This can be literal, where a man actually takes the risk himself for her sake. It is more often symbolic, with his presence creating in her the strength to live a little "dangerously." What a man gives a woman here is a form of emotional support that she can neither give herself nor get from her lady friends, at least in sufficient measure.

The exaggerated form of the male way — the warrior — does not appeal to the great majority of women although they are thrilled by its image in fiction and the performing arts. They want to see the male principle applied to good ends and they cannot help being drawn to the male who does so. Such aims in the male are closer to how they see their own creativity which is, of course, clearest in their role as life giver. The idea of life giver goes to more than childbirth. It includes the life a female rouses in anyone she chooses to give herself to, whether as a lover, a friend or a mother. That a woman sees so much of the life giver in herself is one powerful reason why she so adores a man who wishes to contribute to the general good. Such an attitude in a man makes her feel that he is more likely to work with her on what she finds worthwhile and fulfilling.

It is inherent in male energy to change the world, often in dramatic ways. The male way moves quickly and with commitment to its goals and is ready to clear whatever may stand in its path. Women find the male's actions and sense of purpose breathtaking, especially when they are given to constructive or socially worthwhile ends. Women see in men a way that they want to make their own and they happily accept that the only route to do so is in a love relationship with a male. Their admiration for the male way and their longing for it is rooted in how the more directed and focused male energy makes women feel "together" and right with life and the world. Women asked to describe the feelings they want men to give them — in the present sense — use, in addition to the word together, words like whole, grounded, complete, at ease, settled and so on.

Female intuition and the rich emotions that feed it can become so intense that they carry a woman away, making her feel lost in space and disoriented. For most women it happens too often that their energy becomes too diffuse, leaving them its servant rather than its beneficiary. It is difficult for most men to get the sense of how diffuse a female can feel when her ways go off on their own. You can grasp some of it by trying to combine a feeling of hopefulness with being confused. Or you can two select feelings, one which pulls you together and the other dividing you, such as the wish to love and being ambivalent. At such times, and between such times, women look to the male way as the natural complement to the short side of their own. They see in the male way a sure hope of consistently feeling grounded and centered.

A lovely young woman of great emotional color, call her Ariel, wanted to work on how her emotional surpluses were scaring men off. Ariel's issue suggests a point Freud often made about how looking at an extreme can make things easier to see in the usual case.

Ariel: Do men know how good it makes a woman feel to see how much they want to be with her? Sometimes I think that men feel we have all the marbles because we're the ones who say yes or no. And the men, they're always ready! The men, the men, they feel so good to be with!
AFB: A woman's beauty can easily overwhelm a man.
Ariel: Form or feeling?
AFB: Both.
Ariel: Well, I have enough of form and too much of feeling!
AFB: It's unusual for a woman to complain about her charms.
Ariel: I have no problem with my looks. They work well at getting things started. It's what happens later that concerns me. (pause) I feel more like myself when I have a guy to care about. Compared to me a man has slow feelings. That difference means a lot to me. When I get carried away emotionally I can look at how cool he still is and feel better. That's where the problem starts. He has to want to be there.
AFB: Do you tell the man you care about how much his way helps you to feel good?
Ariel: Mostly I defend how emotional I am. I'm all apologies because I know men don't like it.
AFB: Men feed off of female emotions. They make men feel more alive and confident.
Ariel: Too much of a good thing is not good.
AFB: Why not tell the fellow you care about what his presence does for you. Men like to help women and

when a woman asks for help very few men would want to say no.
Ariel: Maybe I should ask for more by letting him know how much good he's already done just by being there. But how do you tell a guy thanks for putting up with my hysterical ways?
AFB: Sell the positive. Tell him about how good his steady way feels in your life. Let him know that you feel centered and more in possession of yourself when he is there. Men like to hear things like that.
Ariel: That makes me feel manipulative.
AFB: If it's true then it's not manipulative at all. It feeds the relation and in a healthy way.
Ariel: If I could make a guy comfortable with being there for me, then I would have what I want.
AFB: And he would get all those good feelings back a thousand times over from you.
Ariel: Is that ever true!

You are the main event in women's lives. Women look to you in hopes of finding the poetic ideals they long for, just as men look to women with hopeful images that are also best called poetic. Men, sensitive or otherwise, see the female as a majestic voice of what is beautiful and sublime in nature, and women see the male as majestic in living nature's power to reshape all things. If the male's power were represented by a waterfall and its rapids, then the female could be its mist carrying off life giving water and creating a rainbow for all to see. The main event of her life is for your strength to frame her life giving ways with a trustworthy sense of grounding and direction. This is one of the richest meanings behind the once popular expression "It's so nice to have a man around the house."

Women want to feel more in charge of themselves. They usually have the comfortable feeling of being at the center of their intuitions, but things can be different with their emotions. The great majority of their emotions are wonderful pluses to them and to men. Women are, however, vulnerable to their own ways becoming overdone, stealing their composure and leaving them feeling off balance. Perhaps nature has done this as one of many ways to make the male still more attractive to the female. Whatever nature's ruse may be, a woman's vibrant ways give men more than enough reason to want to be with her. Her joie de vivre and easy, intuitive sense of things are just two of the feminine wonders that compel men to seek a woman out. A woman is seduced on her side by the male's steadier way and resolve, things she sees from the first in his thicker frame and greater muscle bulk. Your loving feelings for her and your eager wish to be with her make her feel as if contained by you and your strengths. This gives her the settled feeling she very much wants of being centered by your energy. This gives her such a rich contentment that she can only wonder how best to do likewise for you.

The creation of two sexes is one of nature's most remarkable works, if not the most. The mind of nature on male versus female is for the distinction between them to be happily dissolved away in relationships. Nature has it that a woman's presence works to awaken more and more of the feminine part of yourself and yours to awaken her masculine part. Each gender has the other gender to a lesser degree and nature has made the sexes for relationships as a means to energize and expand that lesser part of each. When a couple feels that each is so, so right for the other it likely that each is feeding off the other this way.

When a woman sees the vigor and power of a male in action she feels thrilling emotions that lift her up high and can easily carry her away. The phrase immortal male captures how she then feels because he fills her with a life giving exhilaration. This power and vigor are in the most ordinary actions and show in every little thing you do. It can be no more than how deftly or decisively you walk, or move, or posture yourself. It could be the way you do your work, or even the pensive look you take on as you consider what actions to next take. Wherever she finds it she sees the sure and certain ways that go with putting action over emotion, a thing that does not come as easily to her. A female is a male's understudy and eager companion when it comes to the mastery of thinking and acting over feeling.

The power to rise above emotional energies and to remain focused on your purpose or goal is at the heart of what women regard as the immortal male. A woman longs to have the male way in her life and her rich emotions and intuitions easily tell her that she can only secure this, her lesser part, in a relationship with a male who cares about her. The next time you may feel that a woman has too much leverage in dating or love, think about what she hopes to get from you. Her coy ways are her means of telling you how eager she is to enjoy what you have to offer her. And the more she watches you struggle to remain composed before her charms, the more she will admire your male way doing its thing before her very eyes and be charmed herself.

GUIDED EXERCISE. Use visualization to learn more about how your male energy affects a woman, making her feel more "together" and better oriented. Imagine a woman you wish for on a sailing ship with no captain, moving by the will of the water. Step into the images that come to you and feel their experience.

GUIDED ANSWER. "I see a large sailing ship. There is no captain on it and it just drifts freely with the current and the wind. The passengers don't know where they are going and feel out of control. They are looking to each other for assurance. I see a woman I would like to meet. I'm drawing near to her and stepping into her image. She looked more composed on the outside than I find her on the inside. I feel fear taking hold of me and it is hard to stay on top of it. I want someone, a man, to hold me and tell me all is well. I want someone, a man, to tell me what is happening and make me feel in charge of myself again.

"Out of nowhere the captain appears. The passengers see him and begin to feel hope and relief. I am stepping again into the woman as she learns that the captain is on board. The negative feelings of fear and apprehension are subsiding. In their place I feel hope, joy and a growing sense of ease and comfort. I feel more the master of myself now that I know the captain is here. I am watching the captain go to work putting the ship about. I sit down to enjoy feeling settled and secure again. I feel grateful to the captain for restoring the ship."

You can feel what your male energy does to females by looking at some figures from Greek mythology. Try the titan Prometheus, or gods like Apollo, Zeus,

Poseidon and Vulcan; mortals and part mortals such as Hercules, Achilles, Ulysses, Hector, Jason and Agamemnon may also help. Male figures in movies with themes of Camelot and heroism also work. For example, Kirk Douglas in the heroic movie Spartacus captures the feeling very well.

Chapter 15.

Around and Through Female Ambivalence

Will you, wo'n't you, will you, wo'n't you, will you join the dance?

...from Alice's Adventures in Wonderland by Lewis Carroll

It has been said many times and in many places that it is a woman's prerogative to change her mind, or even to be unable to make up her mind. Some men feel that this is a privilege women overwork. Some men even see uncertainty as central to a woman's nature, though that overstates what can become of their emotions. Trouble's afoot when the female you fancy isn't sure she fancies you. But is it really trouble? The fact is, you have here a fine opportunity to put your male energy to good use and win her fancy, and more.

Every good in nature becomes less desirable when it is over done and twice so with personal qualities. For some men there is the risk that in working too much at being masculine they will become emotionally insensitive. It takes a little more effort for a male to see the down side of feminine excess. Many women get lost in their intuitive emotions and become cloud borne. When this happens they search for meaning everywhere and arrive nowhere. Their otherwise rich and guiding emotions fail them for want of center and then they feel spacy and lost. At such moments they will want you to pull them in and find themselves grateful for what your male energy does to them. Women want men to solve the problem of their ambivalence and are drawn to men whom they feel will do so. Getting them to resolve their uncertainties, or simply getting them out of a foggy emotional state, appeals to them on a number of levels.

Chapter 5 noted the wisdom of persistence and how it appeals to a woman's need to watch you discover her. The efforts involved in persisting also give her a proof of your trustworthiness that she respects, and this works to open her to you even more. It pays to persist with an ambivalent woman that you want to get to know. It pays to persist on an informed basis, and the key is to power through her ambivalence. To power through means what it says — to keep on keeping on. Do it nicely because you don't want powering through to become plodding through or badgering. Persevere in trying to disperse the mist of her ambivalence with your good willed resolve to get to her. The idea is to pleasantly put the power and focus of your male way before her because that is exactly what she needs when in such a state. She will greatly admire your male decisiveness at such times. She will also be grateful for it and, as Casanova often noted, gratitude is never far from a woman's affection. It is even better than this, for as suggested in the prior paragraph, women want to be grateful to you for the good things you do to them.

Powering through does not mean you should be sycophantic or become a nagging presence. It is enough to let her know in a polite and gentlemanly way that your interest is sustained. She will be very pleased with how definite your intentions and wishes are and begin to admire you. Unconsciously she will try to clone the way of your male energy and put it to work on herself, for well she knows that you are the answer to her hopes and concerns. This creates a great advantage for you because your male magic falls off with your distance from her and so she will hunger for you to be close by even if she doesn't say so. It won't take her long to sense that your advances are making her earth borne again and that will make her want you to stay — with grateful rewards for you in mind, of course.

An energetic young man who found women beautiful but mysterious was drawn to an ambivalent female. Call him Max. He wanted to work on understanding women better.

Max: There's a very pretty girl in my water painting class, and she is going to drive me to drink! When I look at her she smiles back at me and makes me feel like she wants to get to know me. But when I go to talk with her she is so elusive. She doesn't say no but she doesn't say yes either. It drives me nuts!
AFB: How do you know she isn't just being polite?
Max: She is too deliberate and seductive. Encouraging too.
AFB: What happens when you try to talk with her?
Max: She gives me a big welcome smile, listens carefully to the first couple of things I say, then tries to shoot off.

AFB: And she does this time after time?
Max: Yes.
AFB: Now you know she's ambivalent.
Max: Meaning what?
AFB: She finds you attractive and interesting. At the same time, something is holding her back from completely welcoming you.
Max: Is it something about me?
AFB: Not likely. It's probably something about her.
Max: Like what?
AFB: It could be many things but what it is doesn't matter. What matters is that if you find her attractive enough to want to date her, then you need to continue. Keep in mind that she really wants you to keep coming back. She also wants you to make up her mind for her.
Max: I don't want to do that.
AFB: Agreed. That won't work if you take it literally. What works is to keep returning to her in a polite way that respects her ambivalence. When she sees your interest and your acceptance of her unsure way, she will find you more attractive. In time she is likely to find you so compelling that she will make up her mind to date you.
Max: This is going to take patience.
AFB: That's why it's called powering through. You have to find her attractive enough to be patient while you make your offer. But you will see her warm feelings for you and her interest in you grow as you win her over.
Max: If I let her go I will keep thinking about her. So I'll do it!

Powering through a woman's ambivalence is a sophisticated technique that is easy to learn. It pays to study her ambivalence enough to make good judgments about it, especially to see when she is more plus than minus about you. It also pays to consider what kind of female deserves your efforts. There is some risk of courting a narcissistic personality who will feed endlessly on watching you knock yourself out. Be vigilant for a woman who likes your persistent labors too much. A good rule of thumb for spotting healthy and reasonable ambivalence is her sincere request that you give her time to think it over, as opposed to her enjoying the proof of your interest too much.

The method of powering through her ambivalence also works when it comes up in a relationship. Here the meaning of your strength of purpose is different. The issue here is not so much a show of your interest in her, a thing she will relish, as in supporting her effort to become clear on something of importance between you. If ambivalence still clouds the matter after talking it out then accept the state she is in and send her your decisive ways. This does not mean giving her your ideas on how things should be between you. It means supporting her ability to come to a clear view of things from her own perspective by putting your directed and focused ways before her. This is, in a sense, showing her but what you show her is not "what to do" but rather "how to do it," and the "it" is left up to her. Her intuition will tell her how much she needs your ways and she will be highly motivated to take them in.

A loving couple presented a revealing narrative on just this point. Call them David and June.

David: We get stuck a lot over little things. It gets to the point where I know how I feel about things but June is still mulling it over.
June: That's true but there's more to it. It would help a lot if David would be more patient about it.
David: Patient! I am patient and you still take forever.
June: That's not what I mean.
AFB: Why not tell David what you mean when you say patient.
June: It's more than just waiting. (pause)
David: Well, what is it?
June: It's the way you wait.
David: What does that mean?
AFB: I think June is trying to tell you that she wants a certain kind of feeling and support from you.
June: If you would support me instead of patiently rushing me, I would go faster. I would also feel very good about what you are doing.
David: How do I do that?
June: Well, you could begin by holding me and making feel that it's alright for me to dawdle. When you are close and patient and accepting then I feel more able to do just about anything!
AFB: She feels good enough about you, David, to borrow your strength.
...later with only David
David: I think I can do this, but it will take time.
AFB: She cares about you. The more you give her the support she wants, the more she will care.
David: I'm not really sure how to do this.
AFB: You have a decisive way she wants. Your issue is how to share it with her. In the beginning, demand less, offer more patience and let your own decisive ways show.
David: How?

Around and Through Female Ambivalence 171

AFB: When you see her go ambivalent, ask yourself what feeling she needs. Then relate to her in that theme.
David: Huh? (pause) I need to think this through.
AFB: I think if you ask her about the how to she will spell it out. Besides, the whole thing will go faster and faster once you get into it.
David: That's good. I think I have a basic sense of this. I think that with her input I can do this.
AFB: Try also to pick up on just how she feels when she cannot make up her mind.
David: For me that will be the hard part. But it's worth learning how to.

These thoughts apply to yourself also. Men fall into the quagmire of ambivalence too, though usually not as frequently or as deeply as women. When this happens to you side with your own dominant male tendency to be firm and dynamic. Begin to power through the episode by first being firm about putting off making a decision. This is a good idea because you are not likely to make a good decision while you are ambivalent. Next put in effort to create the clear frame of mind and mood that a good decision needs by holding the resolve to not decide until your energy clears. Most women cannot clear their energy the way you can as a male, or if they can then they do not succeed nearly as much as you. Women realize this and that is why they would like you to power through for them.

To power through describes a technique from race car driving, as I learned when I went to test drive a sports car. The salesman accompanied me along a twisted and winding country road that he selected to show off the car. As we approached a 30 mile per hour severe turn he said "Take this turn at 60." I looked at him anxiously and he added "Don't worry, it's a deserted road and the police won't bother you". I replied that I was more worried about winding up in the trees than about the police. He laughed and replied "Just power through the curve by accelerating into it. That's what the car is engineered for". I did what he said and it worked perfectly. As the months slipped by my mind worked over that phrase and I found more and more situations where it applied. The technique of powering through can only be considered masculine. It works by holding a person steady in the midst of foggy feelings and indecisiveness. This steals energy from the negative state of indecision and uses it to create a frame of mind and feeling that is more focused and directed. Power through to become clear again when ambivalent and see for yourself. Then try it on the next ambivalent beauty in your life and see what happens.

Around and Through Female Ambivalence 173

GUIDED EXERCISE. Use your imagination to conjure up images for the idea of powering through female ambivalence. Smoke or clouds followed by a strong wind or images of things floating aimlessly in water followed by a strong current often work well for this.

GUIDED ANSWER. "I am high up on a mountain with a beautiful view all around me. I am looking into the far sky for something to stand for female ambivalence. I see airplanes skywriting. The letters are clear and well formed and they spell out the words female ambivalence. The smoky letters are beginning to break apart and become part of the sky. I can no longer see what they spell. The wispy smoke is still there, slowly moving this way and that. This is what my imagination gives me for female ambivalence.

"The idea of my powering through changes the scene. Storm clouds with high winds are blowing to the right of what remains of those letters. The wind blows into the letters and fragments them. Now one large gust swoops in and carries them away. All that remains now is a refreshing, clear blue sky."

Chapter 16.

Wily Women

FIRST WITCH
>Round about the cauldron go:
>In the poison'd entrails throw.
>Toad, that under cold stone
>Days and nights has thirty one
>Swelter'd venom sleeping got,
>Boil thou first i' the charmed pot.

ALL
>Double, double toil and trouble;
>Fire burn and cauldron bubble.

...from Macbeth by William Shakespeare

Some women resent being referred to as foxes. Their resentment is often rooted in a fear of being reduced to only a beautiful object and having their person discarded along the way. Unfortunately, their resentment keeps them from seeing how richly the implied comparison with that creature speaks not only for their striking beauty but also for such personal qualities as elegance, emotional swiftness and grace. Shrewdness and stealth are also among the many other attributes they share with the wily fox, and their subtle ways are still another. A woman can make her presence known in ways that escape men but that reach all the women she wants. She can make herself known to a group in the quietest way but with the unmistakable presence of a vapor or fragrance, and other women quickly get her scent.

When another woman has eyes for the one a first woman is taken with, the message to stay away goes out. Other women pick it up immediately and they may or may not respect its meaning. Many will take it as a challenge because women want to be confident of their ability to win the interests of a man from other women. Jealousy comes quickly and strongly to a woman when another woman is reaching for the fellow the first one cares about or values. A jealous woman has a number of intriguing strategies that she is likely to use. Among the first is to go after the fellow that the other woman really cares about. This strategy avoids the unsavory prospect of a direct confrontation with the other woman and is something of a divide and conquer reply to that other woman. This is an area where women can show extraordinary emotional skill at creating the circumstance they want.

What now follows can easily be a situation you probably would rather avoid, if given a choice. She will make herself available and obvious to him (the fellow that the other woman really cares about or values) and try to draw him in, striking a blow at her real adversary. You can be prepared to sense this when it comes your way. Women do not usually make themselves easily accessible to your affections and you should be duly cautious when it happens. It is only when you have first won them over with what you have to offer them from within yourself that this is expectable. Women want to be emotionally compelled to show their interest because they love to be governed by their feelings. When a woman foregoes that need and reveals her interest too easily or too quickly, you then have reason to ask what is really happening and to be curious about her motives.

How will you know if her flirtation is the real thing or an act of jealousy toward a rival female? For one, if she really is so interested in you that she will be direct and defer some of her need to watch you discover her, then you should have no difficulty seeing that kind of interest coming from her. This means she will be open and honest with you without compromising herself. What's more, in assuming a basically male approach to meeting you she will show signs of the same anxieties that males experience. This will include managed, but perceptible concern with the risk she is taking. Like a man she will sweat over the prospect of rejection but as a woman she will have trouble stifling her much greater concern about not being found desirable. The absence of these two anxieties, and especially the second, is a signal that her motives are questionable. Stress the second because it is very difficult for a woman to put her desirability as a woman on the line.

A similar ploy of a jealous woman is to try to get to the man she really cares about by making herself available to another man. Here a woman is jealous because a man she wants has not show enough interest in her or because of his interest in another female, possibly both at the same time. Her strategy is basically the same and you should be wary of the signs of insincere interest coming your way. She will flirt with you and make it apparently easy for you to connect with her because she wants the male she is really interested in to notice. The telltale signs of her lack of sincerity are in being too easy to be with and not being anxious enough about her outcome. In general, and as already noted, when a woman makes you feel there is little need for the usual exertions of a first meeting, and shows too little concern about compromising herself, you then have good reason to wonder what she is up to.

It is not always easy or even possible to read the emotion of jealousy in a woman, especially if she is new to you. This dark emotion usually does not have obvious and telltale signs the way a happy mood does with its giveaway smile and good cheer. In fact, jealousy usually wants to move with stealth and go unnoticed so as to more easily achieve its goals. Even the hostility often found with it can be difficult to make out if you do not have prior knowledge of the person. The emotion of jealousy can be quite strong and yet show little or no outward sign of itself, at least to those unfamiliar with the given person. However, it leads to actions, often of a subversive or hostile kind, that give it away. This is one area where women favor taking swift and certain action, the way males generally do. A woman foregoing deep concern about her dignity or desirability is likely to be running on jealousy. And again, a woman who has little need for you to honor the usual concerns of first getting to know one another is likely to be up to something unsavory.

A young woman with a pleasing, earthy way was anxious that she had given her heart to the wrong man. Call her Ginger. She used her wiles to find out where she stood.

Ginger: I know Alex about a year now. When we met I was looking for a good guy to care about and I was ready for it. It didn't take long to feel that he was right for me. We got close and fell in love. I wanted to be with him all the time. (pause)
AFB: So far, so good.
Ginger: Not so good now. We were getting closer and closer and then after about six or seven months, it stopped. I didn't know what was going on. At first I let it pass, thinking it was me. But then I realized it wasn't me because it felt like we were losing what we had. I watched his interest fade. We talked about it and he said he cared. It felt like he cared but it also felt like he was going away. I became afraid that I was somehow letting him down.
AFB: How did you think you might be letting him down?
Ginger: Well, I knew I was being good to him because that's how I felt about him. So at first I thought there must be something important to him that I wasn't picking up on.
AFB: Did you ask him?
Ginger: Sure and he said everything was fine. But it wasn't fine. It went on like this for a while and then I began to get suspicious because nothing was making sense any more. (pause)
AFB: Suspicious of what?
Ginger: At first I thought he wanted to go his way and then I decided to just make it easy for him. But he stayed in my life and I liked having him there. Then one day I was watching a movie and it hit me that he might be living that movie. It was about a

man who loved women but who had trouble being with just one.

AFB: Let me get this straight. The movie was about a man who had trouble staying with just one woman or about a man who liked to have several women at the same time?

Ginger: The second. I never found real proof of his being with someone else but I believe what I feel. Besides, when it came to the point of flat out telling him my suspicion he admitted it! That hurt a lot. (pause) My first thought was whether I could feel alright about being part of his harem. Can you believe that?

AFB: That may have been the shock of disappointment.

Ginger: So I took time away by myself and travelled to get my head and feelings straight. When I became clear I found myself loving him and really, really angry with him. I didn't know what to do. And then that same movie came to mind! I decided to do what the woman in that movie did. I would give him a dose of his own medicine.

AFB: Why that?

Ginger: Well, I had a need to get all that anger out of my system. But there was a better reason. I thought that if he could want me as I wanted him, then seeing me with someone else might bring it out.

AFB: So you weren't just out to hurt him?

Ginger: That was part of it. (pause) I knew his habits and where he would get wind of what I was doing. I went to the right places and began to date men. Some of them were really nice and I thought a few times that if I didn't love Alex I could really go for some of them. I didn't do more than date, so don't get the wrong impression.

AFB: So word got back to Alex?
Ginger: Was he ever undone! He never expected a female in his life to play his game. At first he sort of admired me as a peer at doing his thing. It didn't take long for Alex to see what was going on. He got angry once and said I was trying to control him. I said a healthy relationship takes two people, not three or more. He laughed at that, nervously. (pause) He's still thinking it over.
AFB: How does it look now?
Ginger: The good part is that he is obviously afraid of losing me now that he knows I will do what I have to do.
AFB: Meaning what?
Ginger: If he doesn't deliver then I will bite the bullet. I'll end my relation with him, mourn the loss and move on. It will hurt but I will do it to get to better days.
AFB: That's strong medicine.
Ginger: I know, but I'm serious. So now he doesn't really know what he wants to do. He knows he wants me. He knows he's anxious about all this but he hasn't yet said let it be just you and me.
AFB: I wish you luck with this. It sounds difficult.
Ginger: It is. But I don't know what else to do.
AFB: Are you still dating others?
Ginger: Yes, and it helps. It gets my mind off how hurt I feel and I admit it feels good to know it will get back to him. I really just want Alex. I'll wait till he knows what he wants.

Women are highly inventive about securing their interests and safeguarding them from others. They take measures long before odious emotions such as jealousy or rage can enter because they themselves do not like the way such things feel. The virtue of patience runs deep in them and they apply this admirable part of their nature to win the men they are drawn to. They feel, as noted in chapter 7, that they can wait until their soft and subtle message reaches the fellow they are wishing for. They are usually patient with all phases of growth that need careful support and love. For this reason they generally respond with patience when they sense that the man in their life needs some space and they almost always grant him an easy liberty from themselves. But there is more in the background.

A woman's love and affection usually has a mind for monogamy and possession because she sees the latter as part of the care and feeding of the love she wants. So while you have your dispensation consider that something else comes with how reasonably her affection and tenderness give you your leave. There is a patient devotion to a larger purpose of her own in her acquiescence to your need for freedom. Her higher purpose is related to the tension between the tendency of men to long for more freedom and of women to long for more of monogamy and commitment.

They will discuss this tension with men with whom they are not involved. They will wish that it were otherwise because monogamy and being there always and ever for that one special man feels natural to most women. In the end they do what everyone must do to make life work — they make compromises. They concede that they cannot entirely possess a man so they settle for the most important parts of him. Men, on their side, give up some of the need to feel free and learn to give more of themselves to her and to show her more devotion, especially in obvious ways. The issue for men is usually to give her more of their emotional life, a thing that makes women feel that men are anchored to them because that is what giving him their emotions does to them. The issue for a woman is often to learn that a man's need for liberty does not mean he is not devoted to her or that he plans to compromise, hurt or abandon the relation. The woman's issue is more difficult than the man's because it is at cross currents with how strongly she wishes to give herself to the relationship.

GUIDED EXERCISE. Experience some female wiles for yourself. Recall a woman whose heart felt threatened and who took measures to do something about it. Use visualization to take on her experience.

GUIDED ANSWER. "I remember seeing a plot like this in a movie. A beautiful woman who cared deeply about a man became jealous when another women tried to win his interest. I can see the hard squint of her eyes and the angry flaring of her nostrils. I'm drawing close to her and see her pulse on her neck swelling up and down with anger. I'm stepping in now. She — I — feel tight and tense. My breathing is heavy and I'm angry, furious with the one who wants him. I know who she really cares about and I will go after him. I have to do this because it hurts too much to not do anything about it. I won't let her get away with it.

"Now I'm afraid I will get lost in my revenge. It's him I care about. Why am I doing this? He hasn't betrayed me. It's all about her. I have to drive her off. I have to make her afraid of losing the man she's giving herself to, just like she's doing to me. She lives with the man she loves but she also wants the I one I love. I will get at her by going after the one she loves. I will give her a dose of her own medicine."

Chapter 17.

Playfulness Never Fails

*If I am not worth the wooing,
I surely am not worth the winning.*

...from The Courtship of Miles Standish
by Henry Wordsworth Longfellow

Most creatures in nature have some form of courting ritual. With higher animals, it is usually a mixture of bragging and seduction, often with males competing for females as the opening part of the ritual. Sometimes, as with some horses, it is straight seduction of the male by the female with the latter flaying her tail in the male's face as a wake up call. At other times it can be entirely bragging and domination with the males bent on intimidating each other. This happens with some apes whose power games establish sexual ranks for the males who then take the females according to their (the males') ranks.

Nature spares little variety with courting and mating rituals. Unlike man, it is often the male of the species who is more richly colored and adorned than the female; birds are an example of this. Animal rituals can be long, complex and even confusing to a human. Yet even these can be simple compared to how baffled men can feel before a woman with whom they wish to connect. Fortunately there are simple and easy solutions to what men often see as a great problem.

Women have treasured emotional images of how the best possible flirtation will take place. They take great delight in their images and live them many times before they meet you. They are well prepared to give their hearts to the fellow who is like their reverie. It pays for obvious reasons to know what their reverie is about. A not so obvious reason to study it lies in how little their most perfect romantic images differ from one female to another. In fact, it does not even matter how far past puberty a female is. This one-size-fits-all-situation means that you have a single success skill, or courting ritual, that will reward you handsomely with most women.

Their longed for ritual has playfulness at its center. It makes a direct appeal to their love of gaiety and their rich instinct for fun and wholesome mischief. Some of the good things that playfulness creates have been noted. For one, a spirit of play chases away the nervousness — yours and hers — that is usually there when you first meet. She takes your sporting with her as welcome proof of the lightheartedness with which you will take chances for her sake. She well knows that the chance you take in flirting with her and your upbeat acceptance of it is already well on the way to winning her. Her spirits and her admiration of you run high when she feels your playful strength lift her from her life's fatiguing cares, just as it gives you playful strength to flirt with her. She finds in this a first certainty of your winning male ways and that you will be there for her.

Playing with her to win the goodness and beauty you see in her creates a much desired feeling that you have found her from among the others. This is a feeling that she welcomes and trusts, and even uses to guide herself. Here as elsewhere, a female takes the good expressions from you to her as coming from what she does to you. When you play with her she takes it as a sign of the joy, fun and happiness that you see in her and want for yourself. This not only makes her want you, but it also makes her begin to feel fulfilled, and the latter makes her want you even more.

Women have frisky instincts. This is true of women of all ages, not just the very young. The wish that men will creatively play with them and lift them up and away from the dull tedium of waiting to a smile and glee is never far from them. Your playful delivery is part of the romantic imagery that they savor and play many times over in their wishful imagination. This is one of the things that writers of earlier centuries had in mind when they spoke of women's vanity. When overdone it is now called narcissism but even then it still comes from the finest part of their nature. They want you to tickle their image of themselves and to invite them to run away with you in fancy, and in real life too! They are wonderfully willing to play and some men misread the opportunity as silliness. Women have their own treasured ways, known to themselves and little known by men, and this is one of them. They prize their silliness highly because they know that it expresses their greatest joys and hopes, for themselves and for you. They also know that the greatest happiness they can give you flows the same source at their silliness, and that is their joie de vivre.

They invite you to play with them before a word passes between you. They will look your way for as long as you do not notice them and then they will pretend it wasn't you. Don't you believe it! Take up their invitation. If you don't respond then they will make themselves more obvious and come nearer to where you are. Failing that, they will draw still closer to you and become even more obvious. For the exceptionally dense they have a way that most men never seem to notice but, if you discuss it with them, they will usually tell you about it. When all else fails and when they still want you to make the first move, they will take to looking straight at you. They won't look into you, just at you as if to say "Well, come over here."

Playfulness is one of those means that can truly take hold of a woman and sweep her off her feet. That's one reason why they spend so much time fantasizing about it and running their romantic images before themselves. It captivates them by appealing to their wish to be transported up and away from the present by a strong gust of pleasant feelings. It offers you the same prospect. The figures of the cavalier, the musketeer and the swordsman are from another time and place. They are, however, all expressions of the sporting energy in you that they long for in play and romance. That is why they are well worth studying and experiencing in your imagination. Playfulness, even without a romantic flair, is a behavior that is acceptable almost anywhere and almost anytime. It makes a basic appeal to everyone's humor with a wonderfully rich mixture of glee, bubbly candor and persistence. And, like every form of flirting, playing with her is best done in public for a number of reasons. She will be delighted over how you declare her desirable in front of others. She will also respect and admire you more than usual for taking your chances with her before an audience. The more openly, and with high self regard, you do this the more certain you can be of success, not to mention all the fun you will have along the way.

Take some time with yourself to see and understand your own playfulness. Ask yourself what kind of female personality would be easiest for you to play with. Next, ask yourself where you would be likely to find such a personality type in numbers. You may feel that a serious minded female would make you feel playful, by making you want to balance her offer with more of mirth on your side. If so, try a bookstore, a university library, a lecture, a health foods store, an adult education center and so on. If you feel that a lively, outgoing female would help you feel and express your playfulness more, then try a happy hour, a sports club, some dances, a tennis party, a pool party, dance lessons and so on. You will know that your skill is growing by the increase in the fun and success you are having. As you become adept at enjoying yourself and your success this way, you will spontaneously find yourself playing with women with whom you wish to connect. In time you will find yourself enjoying your playfulness even when alone.

I remember being alongside a very attractive female in a bakery just when she was placing her order. She was too appealing to ignore and I felt my love of play overtake me. As I stepped up to the counter near her and heard her say "Make that two blueberry...". I smiled and added playfully in her direction, "Give her three". We looked and smiled at each other and, after I noted her pleasure — which I expected — I took my cue adding with glee "Better make it four". She giggled and laughed and then asked of me, "Well, what else do I want to order?" to which I replied with a grin of satisfaction "Whatever you say...as long as I get a part of it". She agreed. This exchange took much less than one minute and she opened to me, awaiting more of the play she so much relished. Play takes hold of women very quickly and it pays to look more closely at what the playfulness can be about.

The fact that I smilingly broke in on her order told her that I found her desirable enough to take a risk, for her sake, in public. This is something a woman can only favor. The playful approach told her that I felt good about myself, her and what I was doing. It also told her that I could probably make her feel those delicious feelings that women know they have and long to share with men. The nature of the tease, to increase her order, told her that I was well aware of how nice her lines were. Why else would I toy with her about eating too many calories? It was a sporting way of telling her that she is so appealing and so lovely that not even some overindulgence could take it away. When she replied "Well what else do I want to order?" she was telling me that she wanted to play, and with me. At bottom, the reason this worked so well and so fast is that it gave her both a good feeling and a promise of more. This is part of the discovery principle for, as noted, a woman will take your playing with her as coming from the playfulness, and other good things, that you first see in her. There are few, if any, things that women savor more from a male in a flirtation than playing. And, what's more, it's fun and excitement on both sides. Even onlookers enjoy it, and eventually you will learn to feed off of their smiles and good wishes for letting them share your fun and live a brighter moment through you.

A serious minded, but fun loving, man wanted to find the playful part of himself. Call him John.

John: I love to laugh. It's easy to chuckle over someone else's wit. The problem is that I don't know how to make others laugh.
AFB: Do you find it easy to have fun?
John: Sure. I like to play a lot of sports. I like social drinking and, like I said, I enjoy another person's sense of humor.
AFB: So where's the problem?
John: Huh? I don't know how to go creative and make someone else laugh.
AFB: Do you know how to make a woman smile?
John: Well, if I showed interest in her and was the first to smile, then I think she would smile too. But that's not funny.
AFB: Being playful is about letting the woman do the creative part for you.
John: How do you do that? That sounds hard.
AFB: What happens when you see a pretty lady you'd like to get to know?
John: I wish and then I get anxious.
AFB: Why do you wish for her?
John: Because I know it would feel wonderful to be with her.

AFB: Start there.
John: Where?
AFB: At wonderful. Look at how she makes you feel good. That's where you'll find your first smile. What takes practice is not finding the smile but in getting it out. Let's try it now. Recall a female that you would like to get to know.
John: OK, I have her image.
AFB: What feels good about her?
John: She's nice to look at. She has upbeat ways and a happy, bouncy walk. She's perky and looks a little daring.
AFB: You're smiling.
John: I know.
AFB: Let the smile talk.
John: Huh?
AFB: If the smile had a voice, what would it say?
John: Well, something like "Gee, you look like you would be fun to be with."
AFB: Less serious.
John: I'm stuck.
AFB: What can you picture her doing that would be fun?
John: I can see her on swings, looking really fun and sexy.
AFB: Tell her.
John: Tell her what? That I can see you on swings, looking really fun and sexy?
AFB: Let that image of her lift your face into a playful grin and try something like "You know, I can see you on swings." Say it quickly and with your smile in your voice.
John: I can see why I should smile, but why quickly?
AFB: She will take your quick speech to come from how much she excites you. Saying it quickly will energize you and help to lift your mood into play.

Playfulness Never Fails 193

John: You're right. If I do it in my head, using her image, I feel my mood go up into fun and laughter.
AFB: And when you give it to her she will take it as something she created in you. Women take just about every good thing you offer them as coming from what you see in them. Take her play, her merry way and give it back to her. She will love you for it.
John: I want to try this by myself a few times before I use it.
AFB: It's a good idea to practice beforehand and to wake up the playful part of yourself.
John: I want to have some fun with this and see where it goes.

Some men begin, like John, with a conviction that playfulness requires a creativity that only a select few have. Everyone has the instinct to play just as everyone loves to laugh. The creative part of play is in what comes naturally to you when that lovely lady puts a sparkle in your eye. You can learn how to use your playful instincts to create more of the success you want. Begin as in the dialogue above. Picture a female that you would like to be with. Follow the good feelings that her image gives you and then put those feelings into words.

Note that the creative part of this procedure comes from the female you are wishing for. Her image gives you the good feeling she wants to hear about from your lips, and this is the most important source of playfulness in flirting — not your imagination. Enjoying what she does to you and finding images for the excellent feelings she gives you are gifts from her to you. The part that takes practice is in letting your feelings find their own words.

A good first effort to learn how to use your playfulness is to picture yourself telling her, literally, how she makes you feel. This means brushing up on your word skills so as to be able to craft a sentence that describes what she does to you. Once you feel adept at this, go to a next level where you are less literal. You can do this by following more of the images that fit the good feelings she gives you, and then going on to expressions that speak the feelings.

For example, if she makes you feel like it's wonderful to be alive, then a literal first effort would be a sentence like "Looking at you makes me feel like it's wonderful to be alive" or "Looking at you makes it wonderful to be here." These are statements any woman would love to hear, as long as you mean them. A next effort would be images of how you see yourself enjoying her. If she makes you feel like dancing, then give her that image with something like "I can see myself dancing with you" or "I can see you lighting up a dance floor." If your images are about energy and excitement, similar to what a concert does to you, then tell her with something like "Looking at you makes the music go on" or "I see music in you and I love what that does to me." None of these suggested expressions is highly imaginative, and that is as it should be. What counts is that you playfully send her the happy excitement she creates in you, and for this even the simplest expression will do.

There is more on the relation of what she does to you, to how you can connect with her in Part IV. For

Playfulness Never Fails 195

now, begin by looking at the welcome feelings she gives you, then go to images that fit your feelings, then to expressions that fit your images. Practice until you feel comfortable enough with your play to serve it up to the next female who tickles you. And be sure to let the smile in your delivery tell her how just how good she makes you feel!

GUIDED EXERCISE. Wake up and enjoy the playful part of yourself! Begin by recalling times when you were playful. Recall a woman you would like to meet and visualize how her cues wake up your playfulness and invite it to her. Follow what your play does to her feelings and yours.

GUIDED ANSWER. "I become playful on Friday afternoon, when I begin to look forward to the happy hour. Just the thought of a social drink or two begins to loosen me out before I go. People tell me that a cheshire cat grin comes over me and I start to chuckle. There's a foxy woman I would like to get to know. She is often at the happy hour. When I look at the signs she is giving off, her cues, I get the impression that she's a woman with verve, who really likes to try new and exciting things.

"Her image makes me feel like I would like to try new and exciting things too. I feel a lively, risk taking energy come over me as I look at her. It's the same energy I see in her and does it ever feel good! The playful feeling she gives off makes me want to tell her that I would enjoy doing some racy things with her, like going crazy over some amusement park rides or something really insane, like sky diving. She becomes all smiles and glows with pleasure as I tell her these things. The more I play with how she makes me feel, the more she gives me her lively ways and that makes it so much easier to relate to her."

Chapter 18.

Casting Sexual Spells

*If the rascal have not given me medicines
to make me love him, I'll be hanged.*

...from King Henry the Fourth, Part I
by William Shakespeare

Nothing makes women feel more powerful than to see how their sexuality can rearrange a man. It bends men to them and makes men their willing servants and often their foolish worshippers.

Women learn early in life to come to social encounters with the assumption that the great majority of men will come to them. They feel in charge of their interactions with men and in many ways their feminine emotional edge and deep intuition make it so. The male way of taking action, often of an impulsive kind, feeds their assumption too.

Most of the men who seek women out approach them with high hopes and healthy intentions. Men usually come to women with a willingness to meet their wishes in order to gain their affections. For many men this adds up to feeling that women have all the marbles, at least early on. In the process of meeting many men wish that the shoe could be on the other foot, at least some of the time. Men often feel that nature would be more in balance if the leverage could go both ways. The good news is that the leverage does go both ways because men can undo women just as much as they undo men.

The ways to rearrange them, for a change, are among the most exciting and satisfying things in life for a male. They are natural expressions of what is masculine and they are easy to master because they are natural to the male. This is one instance where being yourself, and firmly, can pay immense dividends. The basic idea is to let the part of your nature that females have less of show and to play to their hunger for it. Adjectives like sensual, stirring, chemical and passionate go with the actions you need to put the shoe on the other foot and make her wonder how to win your favor.

Women bring a sense of challenge to their first meetings with men, and they very much savor it. On their end, it's a game of show and tell. This means that they expect what is good and worthwhile about them to be obvious to you but that you have to work to reveal your worth to them. It's a good idea to make the same demand of them. Let her know, not in what you say but in how you say it, that you want her to reveal her worth to you. This is a playful request and is a first step in casting a sexual spell because women assume their sexual power over men will spare them much effort. If you question that power — nonverbally — then they feel driven to make it show in some fitting way because they value their desirability to the point of wanting to take it for granted, if not needing to do so.

A woman is quick to sense your meanings from the very first. They, your meanings, are in how you present yourself. There is little, if anything, in the way of your verbal and nonverbal cues that a female will not sense and respond to. Some of these tell her how she excites you and some say how delectable your company would be. Both messages are important to women. If you let your excitement show too much then they feel there is little challenge left for them; you've given the game away, so to speak. It is wiser, and better emotional bargaining, to prize yourself more and make them work for you. The more you value yourself the more and the harder they will work to show you their worth. It was once popular to call this being hard to get. It is not just a woman's ploy and, in fact, it improves a man's chances with women more than vice versa because women do not expect it from men.

When you insist, in a playful and dignified way, that she show you her worth, she takes this as the voice of your high self esteem. This makes her value you more and want to give you the proofs you seek. It also makes her want to open to you because her desire to have and experience your male way begins to flood her, if not overtake her. Those adjectives given earlier for your male ways — sensual, stirring, chemical and passionate — go to work on her with no further effort from you. This is especially so when you nonverbally request that she give you proof of her worth, for she assumes that the exertions of a first meeting are on your side, not hers.

Women feel a rush of excitement when you draw near to them. It's a feeling that they love and can never get enough of. The mere sight of your first movement toward them will create all kinds of excited body movements that they wish you won't see. Watch how their shoulders move as you approach them, almost like they are rubbing their spines with their shoulder blades. Watch their heads go up and back, their eyes grow wide with an expectant smile and their breath go away just as you approach them. Many purse their lips as you draw near them, vainly hoping to hold back the signs of high excitement that the sight of you creates in them. They cannot hide what you do to them, as much as they want to. There is a power in you they are wishing for and, when you are within a few feet of them, they feel great excitement as your energy crosses their body boundary and touches them. This is a moment of their undoing.

Your power has many faces and well they know it! It is a power to be more directed and more focused than they can. It is a power to be closer than they can to risks and even to danger without becoming undone. It is a power of self mastery that puts you more in charge of yourself, and especially your emotions, than they can be. It is difficult to exaggerate how much their being near your male way arouses their interest and triggers their chemistry. Every male has this power or else he would not be a male. Women cannot feel it and not also feel waves of sexual excitement at the same time. Women cannot feel it and not also relish images of you touching them, holding them and being close to them.

Use your emotions and gestures to tell her that you will light up her life with the wonder of your ways if she will show you that she has equal wonder to offer you. Make her feel that she must work to win your esteem and high regard for what she is made of, even for how beautiful she is. The harder she tries to win your interest the more exciting and worthy she will find you. Just make sure to be generous with your show of interest and enchantment over her, every now and then, for a female cannot take nearly as much emotional withholding as a male. Her delicate nature on withholding is one of many reasons why she so needs, and admires, the man with heart enough to try his luck on her.

There is more to the story than show and tell. Like the important distinction between what you say and how you say it, there is also your delivery. Being sexy is a form of communication. The way you look and move reveals how much in touch you are with your own sexuality and how well you feel about sharing it. Male energy can send a message into a woman telling her how exciting he is. You can make a woman wild with excitement by doing this. How do you do this? By letting your desire for her show without being explicit in words or with any large body gesture. Let it tell in your eyes, your movements, your expression, the way you flirt by moving first closer to her and then away, without touching her. Do this in a measured way, holding to your need to see her tip her hand, because your restraint speaks for your worthiness in her eyes. Being measured will also make her feel that you are acting on her behalf, showing restraint because you value her. By showing your value for her this way, you will also avoid making her feel overwhelmed or worse, anxious. Assuming a measured approach sheds light on why women like playful shyness in a man, for they feel that its charmingly boyish way can only invite the best and most welcome feelings they can have for a man.

The entire process of using your nonverbal, sexual cues to make a female want to show you her worth is very fast. The whole thing can put women into a feeding frenzy of interest in only a few minutes. The cues, or signals, are swapped that quickly once you have insight into what you are doing and how she is responding. This is another variant of women's need to be discovered. What's new is that here you don't ask, you demand, so to speak by carefully withholding your best regard for her pending a show of her interest in you and some signs of her worth. Your trustworthiness is here too in your ability to withhold your sexuality from her pending more from her — an event that commands instant not-to-be-argued-with respect from her. Women have trouble believing that a man, any man, can say no to an offer of their affections. This kind of posturing and presentation with a female who delights you is the sort of thing that a native American might call powerful medicine, and it is. Study it carefully and you will succeed in putting the shoe on the other foot.

A woman becomes increasingly vulnerable as her interest grows. The male who can send himself into her sexual emotions in the manner described here can diminish and even shut down much of her most powerful needs — to be found or discovered, to trust, to support and be supported in her purpose. A blindness can come over her so that all her needs collapse into giving herself to this one transporting experience. Her rapture has at least two sides. One is her need to prove her worth and, when you are skilled at this, it is the lesser. The other is a genuine rapture with your sexuality, offered in a wholesome way that bypasses anxiety in her. Again, the offering should be by gesture and expression, that is nonverbal, because the implicit is both more powerful and more socially acceptable. Much of this rests on a basic difference between the genders in sexual excitement. While men can be much more impulsive than women at the beginning of a sexual tryst, women can become much more lost to their interest as it grows. When women choose to give up control, they really give it up!

There is a point of theory worth citing on how the coming together of power and sexuality in the male can spellbind women and simply and utterly put them beside themselves. The energies of the two major drives in man, sexual and aggressive (mastery), are not entirely separated. There are points where they become difficult to see as separate, and passion is one place where the distinction blurs. Women feel an extraordinary, cosmic sense when their arousal draws them so close to a man that they feel his aggressive male energy running together with and into his sexual energy. A woman begins to merge with a man as his energies begin to merge with one another. This is her natural way of experiencing his arousal and excitement. Women see their nature and ways as setting in motion this great movement of men's energies toward each other and very much want to be swept away by it. This means that a woman releases a flood of feeling, in herself and her lover, because she wants to let it carry her away. Among the reasons for her deep wish to be carried away is that she takes the male's passion as her handiwork, meaning that a woman can only admire and take pride in the sexual effect she causes.

As for the aggression itself, that powerful drive for mastery that women so admire, there is little to suggest that they are aroused by the prospect of being its object. Their thrill is with the sense of safety and power that your presence gives them, whether or not a real risk is present. When you are near a woman, she cannot help keep her inner images from scenes of you safeguarding her security and making her feel that all is well with herself and life. Most men know how romantic it is for a woman to feel that their presence enables her to take, and enjoy, risks she would otherwise avoid. That is probably why Hollywood has worked its image well, especially its exaggeration in the figure of the motorcycle gang. This image often succeeds in displaying how aggression can be sexually exciting and vice versa, though here aggression moves from the idea of mastery toward destructiveness. With or without the entertainment value of antisocial behavior, this Hollywood theme makes the relation of sexual excitement to aggression easy to see, and that shortens the distance to learning to use it for your success.

The relation of sex to aggression in the personality is a useful fact of nature. It is especially useful in succeeding because women become sexually interested only after first seeing that your aggressive powers are healthy and serving worthwhile ends. What you probably take for granted as a male — the ability to hold to your aim or goal above your feelings — is a form of mastery that females have less of. When a female sees this in you, and also feels that you have good ends in mind, she quickly feels a rush of sexual excitement. This means that as you become more aware of how women respond to your more evolved instinct for mastery, you will see that you cast a first spell over women simply because you are a male. When a female sees your mastery expressing your wish that she show you her worth, as outlined earlier in this chapter, she has little choice but to feel that she must be yours. When you express your natural mastery openly, and with self regard, then women willingly fall into line with it. It cannot be otherwise for women seek such things in you before they even meet you.

According to Freud there is an innate masochism at the bottom of a woman's excitement over male strength. There are even women who agree with him on this in spite of his sexist reputation. Freud felt that women are more inclined than men to find pleasure in pain, in a number of ways. The idea is debatable but it is worth considering as you try to understand some of the choices that romance minded females can make about men.

Freud's idea makes sense of that most avoidable of women, the "bitch." Her surface behavior seems to have male distress as its goal but what she is really after is provoking the male into doing it to her. Her gains, in Freud's view, are a masochistic pleasure and relief of unconscious guilt. The latter because pain usually relieves guilt, and the relief is felt as pleasure. Strange as it sounds, the idea is that the man who hurts her on one level gives her even greater pleasure on another. Right or wrong, Freud's ideas are profound and, in my view, worth some thought because they can help make sense of some female choices that seem to make no sense at all. As for the figure that his ideas try to explain, stay away from her. Saucy is one thing but calamity is another.

Freud's notion of female masochism also puts more sense into why females long for you to play with them. Teasing is a form of playfulness that has a healthy relation to masochism because teasing gives her play and some thrilling hints at danger at the same time. The play and thrill in teasing move toward success as long as they are not overdone. They move even more quickly to success when added to your gentle demand that she show you her worth. Loading your demand with this kind of play can tickle a woman silly and lead to very rapid success.

A woman, call her Sally, whose form fit one of her occupations was concerned about issues of seduction. She was a white collar professional by day and a provocative dancer by night. She spoke to the point.

Sally: I often laugh to myself while I'm dancing. Most men don't know what they do to women and there I have them eating out of my hand. It's really easy to excite them because men think with their, uh, you know.
AFB: And women don't think with their, uh, you know.
Sally: Sure, but few men realize it. When I'm dancing I have to laugh at how the men in the audience just give it all away. They have no idea what they can do to women, at least the ones who come there.
AFB: So are you wishing that you could meet a man who knew this?
Sally: Of course! Why do you think I dance at night?

AFB: Huh?
Sally: No, I don't think I'll meet him there. I dance at night because I know what a nice guy with that kind of smarts could do to me. It would be instant seduction and I wouldn't have much of a chance. But, when I dance, I'm the seducer. It makes me feel better, you know, in charge.
AFB: So you feel vulnerable to men who can see women's sexual desires.
Sally: Most men don't and they just give themselves away. But the ones who see it, they have much more control over me.
AFB: You dance to take back control?
Sally: No one wants to feel so vulnerable. Like I said, dancing makes me feel in charge.
AFB: What happens when you meet the kind of man who can do this?
 Sally: It's happened a few times. I lose it. (pause) I guess the way I feel is that either I have power over him or he has power over me.
AFB: No others options?
Sally: Like what?
AFB: Enjoying what he does to you and going with it. No power struggle.
Sally: Well, I guess I have issues here. I never liked being controlled. But that's something else. (pause) It would be easier to just go with what a guy like that can do. For now I'll keep on dancing and doing it to them.

GUIDED EXERCISE. Discover for yourself what you do to women! This exercise is well worth some extra effort. Use visualization on some scenes where the material of this chapter is portrayed. Begin by recalling what women do to you and then go on to experiencing what you do to them.

GUIDED ANSWER. Here is how this exercise went with a man, call him Bart.

Bart: Alright, I listened to the instructions and I'm ready. Now what?
AFB: This is the cake part. Form a mental image of a woman whom you find sexually attractive.
Bart: This is an exercise? (pause) I have the image.
AFB: What does it do to you?
Bart: You have to ask? (pause) Well, she is really well formed. She's sweet, giving and luscious...and I would give my life for a night with her!
AFB: Now that didn't take long!
Bart: Are you sure this works?
AFB: Hold on to what she does to you. Try to keep those feelings alive while we move on.
Bart: Roger that.
AFB: Go back to the same female image you just used. See yourself returning her provocative sexual cues, the ones from her that got you going, and make her want to work to win your esteem.
Bart: I'm there. I'm letting her see what she does to me and letting her know it's not for free.
AFB: Good. Stay there until you see that you are getting to her.
Bart: Boy is she nice to look at! (pause) My attention is going now to her. I can see that she is getting my

message and wants to show me that she's worth my attention, not that she needs to do anything!
AFB: Good. Get closer to her and then step into her image. Take on her feeling experience as you do so.
Bart: This isn't easy for me.
AFB: It becomes easy when you want it.
Bart: Alright, alright! (pause) I'm there.
AFB: Look at yourself with her eyes and describe what she feels.
Bart: I don't want him — uh me — to see how he makes me feel. He excites me. He makes it hard to contain myself and not rush out to him. I just want to be near him and feel what he's like. (pause) It feels very good in here! (pause) But I'm anxious that he will see what he's doing to me. It's too nice to tell him. The feelings are delicious and I want more.
...some time passes
AFB: Time to come back, Bart.
Bart: Later. (pause) Alright, I'm giving up the images but I would rather stay with them.
AFB: Why?
Bart: Because I like seeing her sweat for a change.

PART III
SPECIAL SUCCESS ISSUES

Part III applies the prior material to show where a problem is really no problem at all and where the real success advantages lie.

Some men actually have an advantage when they think they have a problem. This is true of shy men and intellectual men, both presented here as having an edge over others when these kind of men learn what their ways mean to women. And some men are slowed by their belief in myths such as the power of lines or of being young or wealthy and so on. These and some other popular myths are presented to point more clearly to what women really want and how to use it to succeed.

Chapter 19.

Shyness

*The deepest feeling always shows itself in silence;
not in silence, but restraint.*

...from Silence
by Marianne Moore

Shy men are unusually unaware of the edge they have over other men. Women look upon shy men as offering guarantees for certain kinds of treatment that they like. Women see opportunities to enjoy romance and sexual play with shy men sooner than with others. They also see in shy men an opportunity to offer an emotional support and encouragement that feels very natural to their gender. These thoughts usually bring little assurance to shy men who generally feel blighted by their shyness. The shy man is almost always convinced that he is missing out on a great deal of romance because he sees his ways as holding him up. He usually does not see that his way, when properly managed, gives him more options with women and a commanding edge over most men in the competition for women.

The man who is shy gives a woman a promise that certain of her anxieties can rest easy when she is with him. Women long for close up contact with how a man actually feels. They constantly hunger for more contact with a part of human nature they know they have less of, the male part. Their sense of being complemented by the male and their curiosity over the experience of being a male is among their favorite and usually undisclosed — to men — fascinations. Male energy is exciting and much sought after by women, especially in its more evolved or refined form. Brutish energy, bullying and domination have little appeal for most women. A woman sees a shy man's reserve almost as an exaggeration of civility or being a gentleman. They also see him as sexy. The shier a man is, the more a woman is willing to pardon him some first assertive efforts and to fill in the difference for him. She does this hoping to eventually open him up so that she can feel his male way, a thing she knows is there in his shy background.

Women's perception of shy men tends to be the opposite of how shy men see themselves, for women usually see such a man as a Clark Kent type. This means what it suggests, that a woman well knows that a shy man is keeping his male strength at bay. Women are quick to have romantic images of their ways going to work on the shy man, giving him liberties they won't give most men. Their imagery sees them inviting the shy man's deep inner strength to themselves, and happily so.

It is not true that most women see the shy man as naive. Some women even assume that a man is shy because he already sees so much of a woman's sensual make up that he feels somewhat overawed by it. The reality of shy men is that they are usually highly adept, both emotionally and intellectually. Their sensitive ways often come from the keenness of their feelings and mind. This is something that women know at once and intuitively, though they may be slow to reveal it to men unless asked.

Perhaps the single strongest message from a shy man to a woman is that he has a right regard for her. The runner up is that he will likely be kind and gentle, with much strength in reserve for her. These are two of the shy man's ways that work quickly to put a woman at ease with him. This is a shy man's advantage that is not to be taken lightly, though it is not often easy to get a shy man to agree.

Men who are shy can use their quieter way to their advantage. The first step is study how much women favor it and are drawn to it. A shy man who sees his advantage is eventually at risk of no longer being shy. Once he learns to market his way, because he sees that women are drawn to it, he may become more assertive and lose his edge. Some shy men will relate that they are aware of how women are drawn to shyness in men and then add that it is not enough. Such men are usually deeply concerned with how they get stuck and what to do about it.

The first step remains in place, to study how and why women favor it. Accepting shyness as an asset makes a man more willing to offer it rather than struggle to hide it. A man who knows this will be more comfortable offering his true self, and that is a very good recipe for success with women under any circumstance. One of the easiest ways for a shy man to get to the assertiveness he hungers for is to learn how to let the pretty lady before him do it with him, or even for him. This looks to grow the connection with her through her innate wish to be supportive, and several times over when she is looking for romance, and then several more times again with a shy man.

Whether a man is shy or not, a woman has a longing to pour herself into him. She finds her fulfillment in waking up her lover to more of life in himself, bringing the psyche to life with her emotions and her ways. A man who is shy has much of the demureness that a woman feels within herself and gives her the welcome opportunity to see a part of her own way in him. This makes her both comfortable and adept at bringing him forward to a richer, fuller life within himself. A woman has the further advantage of sensing what male strengths the shy man has within him. She longs for these strengths and is well fitted by nature to seduce them forward in a way that pleases and excites both herself and her lover.

A woman sees what a man, shy or otherwise, can be. It is her way to lure more of her lover's soul forward with a delicious emotional offering. She sees what he can be, she invites it to life by getting her lover to feel for himself how good it is, and then she revels in it as it comes forward from within him to her. Women know this for many reasons, one of which is that men do this to them, but very few men ever realize how immense their effect on a woman is. The shy man does it too. The simple presence of his male way before her eyes wakes up her more sensitive heart and soul to the joy of feeling his power. And she is delighted to send loving wake up calls to him and to watch him grow before her eyes into a better lover and a more fulfilled person.

Your growth is her growth and she is very much aware of this, for this is part of the psychological edge that almost every woman has over men. Nature has made them midwives to the psyche and they are very, very good at it! Yet for all that, nature has given men more of mastery and panache to redefine life and the world. Women know the differences better than men. Women are quicker than men to look to the other gender to fill themselves up with a way they have less of, but deeply want and need. They see more clearly than men that their joy and completeness comes from a loving tie with the way of the other gender. That soul satisfying sense of grounding that women hunger for is something they cannot get enough of by themselves. They look to men, including shy men, for it. And the shy man makes a more inviting offer of it than most others!

John, a somewhat shy man who appeared in chapter 17, brought up some good points on women and shy men.

John: I think that because I'm shy I tend to attract controlling women.
AFB: A controlling woman can still be good to you. Besides, as you turn on your assertiveness she will be less and less able to control you.
John: Doesn't that spell the end of the relation?
AFB: Not likely. What's likely is that she will feed off of you more and the relationship will deepen.

John: So you feel that women like shy men?
AFB: They see shy men as sexy and safe to be with. Women like it when they see that a man's power is in reserve.
John: That's me alright. But I'd rather have it up front and going out to them.
AFB: How about starting by trying to see that most women find shyness charming in men. There are many other pluses.
John: I can do that. But I'm more concerned with getting to be more direct.
AFB: Well, you can only flirt with so many women.
John: What's that got to do with it?
AFB: A flirtation is what, ten or twenty minutes, and then it's over. But a relationship, that's something else. It's ongoing.
John: So I should look to a lover to help me with this.
AFB: I wouldn't call it help. It's part of the growth and fulfillment that comes from two people caring about each other.
John: I think I know where this is going. A woman is more intuitive and emotional than a man. So she'll see more of what I can be than I can and she'll come on to it.
AFB: That's basically it. But I wouldn't say come on to it. It's more like she sees your energy back there, gives it an inviting smile and draws it out to herself. And you grow in the process.
John: Isn't that like a woman mothering me?
AFB: If you offer her your strength when she feels off center, is that fathering her?
John: No. But I don't thinks it's the same.
AFB: When you offer her your support you're doing what comes naturally to caring. If she gets you to welcome your own powers and their expressions, that's caring too, not mothering.

John: Let me think about it. (pause) What about the issue of flirting? I'm still shy and I'm worried about making a first connection.
AFB: Like we said, you can begin by learning to see that women are fond of shyness in men. They find it seductive and it makes them feel safe. They also tend to assume that shy men are decent.
John: (laughing) Anything else?
AFB: Sure. A shy man puts to rest any guilt a woman may have over sex.
John: That could be right. I think I'll begin by looking at how women respond to shy men.
AFB: Just don't confuse low self esteem, or depression, with shyness. A depressed person is usually turned inward and low key. That's not the same as shy.
John: I don't have that problem. My issue is becoming more assertive. But I think that if I can see that most women really do like shy men that I can accept it and be more comfortable with it.
AFB: Good. And later you can watch yourself get close to her and how that draws out the assertive parts of you that you want.
John: That I would like.

John applied himself to observing how shy men interact with women. He had a need to see for himself that women do indeed feel good about shy men, and that is just what he verified for himself. He found that most shy men do not realize that their worst outcome is for women to be charmed or perhaps amused by their shyness. More often he found the outcome to be a mix of women's favor and admiration for the shy man's struggle to rise above it all. He began to offer his shyness more openly to women as a thing he saw they valued and that he could accept as a good part of himself.

In time he moved on to studying how relationships went between shy men and their lovers. Here he made the interesting observation that a shy man and a shy woman can get stuck in a stand-off. Each of them can end up waiting for the other to go from reticent to open. However, a shy man with an average female does well. For as they come to care about each other the female welcomes the sense of respect and decency she assumes the shy man has, and her assumption is usually correct. She also welcomes his male energy and more powerful ways as a good, safe and wholesome part of him. She more easily relates to those parts in the shy man than in the not so shy man because she finds the shy man's way similar to her own. She also finds it non-threatening.

John found, most of the time, that the shy man's outcomes with a lover are satisfying. He also found that the shy man has an easier time of it because the female is delighted to be there for him as he learns to use and express more of himself. The shy man's bottom line is to have a commanding edge with women because his way makes a woman find him trustworthy much faster than otherwise. A woman assumes that a man is shy at least because he is astonished by how much beauty and seductive power he finds in her. These are things for which a woman can only want to bless a shy man with her admiration and affections.

GUIDED EXERCISE. Learn what your shy part does to women. Go to a time when a woman made you feel shy. Recall your own experience and then step into hers with visualization.

GUIDED ANSWER. Here is a sample reply to this exercise from a chronically shy man. Call him Phil.

Phil: Finding a time when I was shy is easy because I am always shy with women.
AFB: Then go to the last time it happened.
Phil: That was yesterday.
AFB: Relive your experience, the whole thing, from beginning to end.
Phil: I saw this very attractive and sweet gal coming into my building just as I was. It wasn't the first time. I smile at her, she smiles at me and then I get stuck. She is so nice to look at! And she looks like she would be so nice to be with. But I don't know what to do next. My smile becomes frozen and there she is smiling back, maybe even waiting for me. Then nothing.
AFB: Stay with your own experience until you get restless.
...a little later
Phil: It's time to move on.
AFB: Get closer and closer to that lovely lady. Get so close that you can see her nostrils move with her breathe and feel her body boundary reach you.
Phil: I wish this were real! (pause) This is sort of scary because I can just about feel her feelings.
AFB: Now step into her and take on her experience as you were smiling to each other.
Phil: Stepping in. (pause) She sees that I'm anxious.
AFB: How does she feel about you?

Phil: I — I mean she — has warm and welcome feelings for me. As her, I like his smile coming at me. (pause) He's shy, maybe I should speak to him first. It would be easy to talk with him, maybe put him at ease. But I want him to get past it and show me more than a smile. (pause)

AFB: Stay there and let her wishes come to you.

Phil: I — she — feels that it must be hard to be shy and to want to connect with her. I like how he struggles because it makes me feel that he finds a goodness in me. He must be a decent guy if I make him feel shy. I wish he knew how I feel. I wish he knew that I want him to say something, anything! He looks so nice and cute, I would make it easy for him.

AFB: Do you like how she feels?

Phil: Uh huh!

AFB: What are you going to do about it?

Phil: Practice some more. Then when I get the nerve I will get past smiling to talking. But that won't be easy.

AFB: It will be easier as you learn how much of her your shyness has already won.

Phil: That thought I like!

Chapter 20.

The Intellectual

It Don't Mean a Thing If It Ain't Got That Swing.

...a song title (1932)
by Duke (Edward Kennedy) Ellington

    The intellectual man's power of mind comes to women as one of the purest and most seductive expressions of male energy and strength. Women simply adore this ability in men and they are always wishing for more of it in their lives. They see in this the ability to hold emotion at bay while giving oneself to clear thought, and then to action. A man, to most women is something of a purer form of life when it comes to holding to forethought or to action with emotion at arms' length. That's the good part. The other part is in Duke Ellington's capricious comment and he does a marvelous job of capturing the majority of it!

    To think and to know are sublime powers, and both genders agree. Females think and know with more reliance than males on what their feelings mean and what their rich intuitions tell them. A man is a marvel to a woman for his lofty power of reason and comprehension that can find its way with little or no feeling.

Time and again the intellectual finds himself simply adoring a woman, with whom he will tend to make an easy first connection, only to be baffled later on by what she really wants. Time and again she will tell him what she wants but he will simply not understand. Her message is not past his intelligence or his reason. The issue is that her message is past his feelings.

It often happens that the thinking man has learned little, or not enough, about understanding life and the world by how these make him feel. A woman is a more emotional being than a man and hungers for men to pique her feelings. Nothing tickles a woman more than a man who can give her affectionate or even seductive feelings in a wholesome way. The intellectual's edge is in doing this immediately to women with his high powers of mind. Eventually his lady will want other forms of stimulation. That other stimulation, as suggested by Duke Ellington's words, comes from her wish to see and feel his feelings. The idea of "That Swing" is not in what he says but in the emotions that come with its delivery.

It would be wonderful for intellectuals if all that women longed for were a robust mind and not also the rich, feeling part of a man. This distinction is a very easy thing for a female to see and can be a very difficult thing for a male to see. The female almost always has a rich and immediate experience of her feelings. She therefore knows from her own self what she is looking for. The intellectual is often not in close enough touch with his own feelings. His difficulty is that he understands her emotional wishes more in the abstract than from his own emotional experience.

Most women see this very easily and try to turn it to good use.

A woman who cares for a heady man will usually give patience and sweet feelings to him. Her patience comes from her affections. Her sweetness is her loving way of giving him a luscious taste of his own feelings by using hers to stir his. Her hope is that a sustained dose of her goodness will help him to find more and more of the very human, feeling side of himself and give it to her. She has her rewards from him while she waits and this is something that Sigmund Freud noticed more than once.

Freud was fascinated by the interplay of the personality that thinks too much with the personality that feels too much and too easily. He called them the obsessional and the hysteric, in the given order. There is mutual gain when these two meet as lovers. It works better when the male is the heady kind and the female too emotionally rich. The gain on both sides is that each gets a large sample of a less developed part of the self from the other. The intellectual gets to enjoy frequent and rich doses of emotion from her and she gets to see and feel what life is like with thought and action holding sway and feeling in the background. This sort of interplay occurs in all love relationships but it is exaggerated between these two kinds of personalities. The female comes to feel more centered and grounded in every case, and several times so when she is too feeling rich and he too heady. The male feels transported by a lively energy he finds in her but not enough in himself.

As noted, the intellectual's issue is not often in making first contact with a female but in what comes of his love relationships later on. In fact, the intellectual usually has an easy time of it when making a first connection because females see his way as not only masculine but simply intriguing. This kind of male does not stop himself at the gates as the shy male does, but he is at risk of his relationships not coming to full bloom or of ending prematurely. The good news is that there is much he can do to make his love life more enjoyable.

The full remedy for the intellectual is to learn to turn on more of his emotional life. Much of this tends to happen by itself because the intellectual usually finds women of rich emotional color very desirable, and rightly so. Such women are the natural complement to his own way and this leads, as noted, to mutual gains for both lovers. The company of emotionally rich people, male and female, in life overall also helps to wake up more of the intellectual's feelings. Emotionally rich males as friends are especially valuable because their more colorful replies to life literally show the heady person another way to see and respond to the same thing. Activities that want feeling rich involvement go a long way to turn on the personality as a whole. Music, dance, acting and similar activities are an enjoyable way to grow this part of the self.

As the intellectual's feelings come to life he becomes more able to see with emotional eyes what his issue is about. This makes it much easier for him to make further progress in becoming emotionally colorful. It also makes the close up lessons available in a love relation more meaningful. Now the heady man can not only see and enjoy his lover's ways but he can also begin to experience much more of his emotional reply to the feelings she gives him. He can also talk about it with her, a thing she will love to do. In fact, she will love him just for bringing it up because feelings are the most important part of her world.

Jump starting the intellectual in experiencing his feelings more and getting his thoughts to talk to his feelings is the key issue. Once begun, this resourceful kind of man usually makes rapid progress with little further help. This was clear to Ron, the young man of chapter 2 who loved Sharon but whose emotional signals were not yet loud enough to satisfy her.

Ron: It's taken me a long time to understand why Sharon felt short changed. She would talk about feelings and her need to be close to me. I would tell her how I cared and I know she saw it. So I was at a loss to understand what was going on. If she knew I cared then what else did she want?
AFB: How do you see it now?
Ron: She wants me to feel when her feelings are coming to me. She wants me to let myself feel what she does to me. She wants me to feel her emotions too. It's all about emotions and having them.
AFB: That's good. What brought you to this point?
Ron: Well, we've talked about it but for me it was just an idea, an abstraction. I heard the words but missed the real meaning. It became really frustrating, so I put it in the back of my head and hoped something would help me to see what I was missing. I tried watching videos with emotional stories, I even sat in on acting classes. This was fun but it didn't help much. Then I thought that maybe I was trying too hard and just let it go.

AFB: It sounds like you had quite a time getting started.

Ron: That's true. But it came to a head one night when Sharon and I were watching a video. There was a scene of lovers. The woman really loved the man but he was cold to her. The story went on and came to a part where Sharon just said that the man loved the woman but didn't yet know it. I asked her how she could see something like that in a video. She said the acting was really good and then said watch the rest of the story. She was right. So later I rewound that video to that scene over and over again! I watched it over and over again, trying to see what she saw. It took a couple of days but eventually it clicked. I was excited and called Sharon from work when it came together. I said to her that she knew the meaning of the feelings that the man was acting out and that's how she knew he loved the woman without realizing it. Sharon said I was right.

AFB: I bet she was happy for you.

Ron: She was. And she saw much more than I did. She knew that I had taken my first step. Soon I began to see emotional meanings that were there all the time but passing me by. I told Sharon about them and was she ever happy to see how I was growing. She helped me a lot to get the meaning of feelings. Sometimes we would just people watch and talk about what we thought was going on between them. She was so much help. Eventually the whole thing began to take place between us and I finally began to get her meanings. That did so much for our relationship.

AFB: Nice story.

Ron: Yes, it is. But do most men with my issue have this much trouble getting started? I mean once I saw the basic idea in life then it came together quickly.

AFB: Different men take different amounts of time to get started. But just about every man who is low on feeling contact has a challenge to get to the first step.
Ron: So I was typical, no?
AFB: Yes you were. So was your outcome.

There are men who are both shy and intellectual. This does not make for trouble twice over although it might seem so at first. The glitter of the intellectual adds to the merits of this man's shyness and makes him even more attractive and desirable to women. What's more, his rich and carefully spun expressions work very well in first meetings with women. His thinking way is more assertive than his shy way and almost always expresses itself in charming terms that rise above his shyness. And women love it! The strength of his intellectual way solves what may be an issue for his shy way and his shyness simply makes his offerings so much more seductive.

Events are similar as he gets to know a female. Here his shyness offers a satisfying solution to what could be a rough road for his intellectual way.

It is difficult to be shy without also having good contact with one's feelings, for shyness itself is a feeling. Shyness is one of many responses to the feelings of beauty, sexuality and wonder that a female gives a male. Shyness sends out its intriguing invitation to women to bring this man's background personality more to life. A female has a larger challenge with the shy intellectual because his experience of his feelings will usually be somewhere between an average shy man and an average intellectual. The woman he charms with his shy way will be charmed, and delighted, even more with the power of his active mind. His double offering gives her many reasons to gladly offer herself to his shy way. What may at first seem to be the risk of two challenges in one is just the opposite, for the shy intellectual is actually a very rich and winning personality.

Women see the intellectual male as remarkable. They find a noble power of mind in him and they know at once that his male energy makes his personality as swift and true as his mind. More than most men, women see that thought precedes action and they lose their breath to the quick and certain actions they know will follow this man's thoughts. Knowing that feelings and actions follow thoughts makes a woman want to give her loving ways to the first, his feelings, and to join the male's lead on the second, his actions. The rarer species of intellectual who is also shy gleams in women's eyes as a gem of nature and they are eager to give their love to all the value they find in him.

Stereotypes want to make most intellectual men shy. This may be true in early life, say around puberty when a male is just getting to know his new and emerging self. However, the fact is that heady ways are a form of male aggression. It is the aggressive work that comes before action and prepares for it. Most intellectual men are not especially shy but tend to be determined and even aggressive personalities. And so the shy intellectual is a jewel in nature that women prize very highly because of his worth and because he is not easy to find.

The Intellectual 231

GUIDED EXERCISE. Experience how a female senses the emotional meaning of things in a different way from the intellectual male. Recall a time when a female got an emotional meaning that you missed. Use visualization to take on her experience.

GUIDED ANSWER. "I told my sweetheart about a former lover who just joined us at work. It made me uncomfortable and I didn't know why because I no longer have feelings for her. At first I thought my sweetheart would be jealous and maybe that's why I was uncomfortable. But I thought it over and I knew that wasn't it. My sweetheart asked how my ex liked it there. I said that my ex seemed to like it a lot. My sweetheart somehow picked up that my ex enjoys flirting. We talked about it and then my sweetheart's expression told me it all came together for her. I asked her what she sensed. She said that my ex probably wasn't sure of just how I felt about her and that she, my ex, was probably anxious about how I would feel with her flirting nearby. I realized at once that my sweetheart was right.

"I'm replaying this in my imagination and stepping into my sweetheart. I see myself talking to her and feel her feelings coming over her. At first I — I mean she — feels that the other woman may still care and I feel flashes of jealousy and anger. But now my feelings tell me that doesn't fit. The other woman cares but in a different way. I feel a kindness and I wonder what it's telling me. The other woman is a flirt but she has good intentions. She's concerned that flirting near my lover may hurt his feelings. That's all it is."

Chapter 21.

Myths: Lines and Ploys

*Thunder is good, thunder is impressive;
but it is the lightning that does the work.*

...from a letter by Mark Twain
to an unidentified person (August 28, 1908)

Why don't you come up sometime and see me?

...from Mae West's lines
in the screenplay "She Done Him Wrong" (1933)

    Myths are usually formed about some kernel of truth. The myth of lines and ploys is formed about the challenge facing men when they take action to fulfill their wishes to be with the women they find attractive or desirable. Lines and ploys make their first appearance at puberty and in adolescence when they are very common in males. Such young males are very aware of how much they desire to be with girls and, at one level or another, they also realize how little they know about what girls want from them. This mix of strong desire and lack of knowledge or know-how results in often comic experimenting based on movies, the media and wishful thinking. Time and again the adolescent will believe another male's story of a line or other contrivance that is sure to win a girl's interest and affection. Some males continue to believe this into their adult life.

If the world of the adolescent trying to win success with lines and ploys were different, then his outcomes might be more to his liking. If girls were different, and not as they are, they would greet lines and ploys with appreciation for the amount of time a male must spend working and reworking them, as well as for the amount of energy devoted for their, the girls', sake. If a female welcomed or appreciated a line or ploy, then she certainly would admire the young male's resourceful effort to win her interest and affection. Unfortunately, young females, or girls, do not often respond this way. They are looking for certain kinds of emotional offerings from boys. A line or a ploy is not close enough to what girls look and hope for, and the same is true of most women.

The meaning of the myth is in how much it reveals the deep and ongoing desires that men have for women. The wisdom in the myth of lines and ploys is that men love women and men often are at a disconcerting loss to understand what women want on a first meeting. A line or ploy is a device the male resorts to in order to manage his anxious uncertainty over what women want. It would be better if he offered the female his anxious interest because she will read it well and be pleased at its genuineness. She will also be pleased at his pluck to master his anxiety for the sake of winning her interest.

Myths: Lines and Ploys   235

There are some times, not many, when a line or ploy works. When this kind of maneuver works its success proceeds the way a joke does. Most of the time a joke amuses by means of a certain something in its delivery rather than in what the joke itself says. This is why the same joke told by two different people can have such widely differing effects. When a device works in flirting the success depends on that certain something in the way it is offered and on little in the device itself. What succeeds is not the prepared line or tactic but something else in the way it is presented. The fact of the matter is that the certain something is what a female really wants and she would be delighted to receive much more of it than of the device. Please refer back to the lines quoted from Mark Twain at the beginning of this chapter. Their intended meaning is in taking a line or ploy to be thunder and the emotional expressions a woman wants to be lightning — the device makes noise but the feelings going to her do the work of success.

There are many reasons why lines and ploys usually do not satisfy the male who uses them. The reasons come together in how they move away from what women really want. A female's most powerful wish when it comes to males is that they, the males, will give her an emotional show of what she does to them. This, again, is called the discovery principle. Females know that the offering they wish for can only be spontaneous. A line or ploy, thought, rehearsed and conceived before even being with her tells her little if anything about what good things she does to you when you are with her. She sees a line or ploy like a piece of history that is unconnected with the moments when you meet and interact with her. A contrivance in place of the natural and unrehearsed emotional offering she longs for leaves her feeling deprived and frustrated. The words of Mae West quoted at the chapter's beginning were chosen because they, together with her bawdy way, make it easier to see this very basic female longing for a man to see her and let it show in his emotional expressions.

The male who succeeds is the male who knows how to let certain of his feelings show. How could it be otherwise when a female is far more a creature of feeling and intuition than a male? She knows what things mean by the way they make her feel and her highest moments come when her feelings are ignited by yours. A line or ploy or any other ruse is not a feeling. True enough, these things show that your interest is there but they do not reveal your feelings to her in any immediate or living way. It would be better to tell a female that you were thinking of using a line or ploy to meet her but you decided against it in favor of flat out telling her how you feel. This would have more chance of success because when you say such a thing your emotional interest in her is also being expressed, and this is exactly what she wants.

Women are ready and eager to find in you what they are looking for, and this is true from long before they meet you. The male who succeeds in his first meetings with a new female wins many positive emotions from her, and all at once. For one, she takes his open expression of interest in her, and his joy in what he sees, as telling on his high level of self esteem. She finds this very emotionally pleasing and finds the wish for more of him coming over herself even more pleasing. Women know that emotional expression does not come to men nearly as easily as to them. That is one reason why they find high self regard in such men, and rightly so. Men are not even apt to freely express with women the masculine feelings they express with other men. When a man comes to her with the kind of emotional offering she is looking for, she is ready to admire him. On the other hand, a woman is likely to assume that a male who uses makeshifts such as lines and ploys is not yet up to this kind of healthy spontaneity.

She finds more to admire in this kind of man — the one who works that first meeting well — than self esteem. She knows that somewhere behind his flirtation there is a concern over his risk of rejection or failure. A woman's heart quickly goes out to the man who gives her upbeat and happy feelings when she knows what other feelings must be on hold behind what she sees, a point noted several times but worth noting again. Among the messages a woman takes when a man uses lines and ploys is that his anxiety over her is too strong. She will feel that you use these contrivances because you do not yet see enough in her to take bolder and more open chances for her sake.

A woman has a need to see and also to feel that what she is puts you into a state of easy and natural emotional expression of just what you see in her. In this sense, a man who uses lines and ploys makes her feel deficient about herself. She will be more likely to feel that she has failed you than that you have failed to see what she is worth. Most of the time a woman leaving a flirtation that fell short will feel that her disappointment reflects more on her than on the male who made an offer. These are delicate matters that strike close to home with women. They are matters that they are willing to share with their women friends and not at all willing to tell men about.

There is an easy opportunity to see for yourself much of what is described here. The feeling of disappointment in herself is easy to see in a female with whom a male will not dance. She will feel that he has not found enough in her to master his reservation and inhibitions. When this happens, she will be more likely to feel short changed by nature than to feel he did not see all she has to offer. The man who knows how women pride themselves on the power of their beauty to inspire men to express themselves emotionally can approach the next pretty lady with more confidence in his outcome.

Among the things that women hope to find in a male's flirtation are good intentions for him and her together. She brings to her encounter with you images of romance and your wholesome respect for her. She hopes to read in your feelings that you look forward to getting to know her, a thing that is high on her list of most cherished romantic wishes. She expects you, as a male, to be impulsive and she hopes that you will be sporting about the way she feels she must put you off, at least at first. These and other fond wishes are also among what she sees as fitting and appropriate. She does not see lines and ploys as fitting or appropriate expressions of your joy and delight in meeting her. When you use such contrivances she will wonder what else may not go with what feels natural to her and she may even become anxious over it. What feels natural to a woman's psyche is the way of her own nature and she wants nature's way for you to be that

Myths: Lines and Ploys   239

you will freely express the rich feelings she gives you. This means that she wants her emotionally expressive nature to ignite a similar way in you so that she can enjoy you so much more.

A laid back young man with a healthy interest in females wondered why his lines and ploys were no longer working. Call him Andy.

Andy: I don't know what's wrong lately. I'm not getting far with girls. It's not like it used to be.
AFB: How was it?
Andy: When I saw someone I liked I would have something ready to say. That would get a rise out of her and I was off and running.
AFB: How is it now?
Andy: Well, I use the same material but it doesn't work like it used to.
AFB: Does it work at all?
Andy: Not much.
AFB: Your mood is somewhat flat. Any problems with depression lately?
Andy: I've been feeling slow and lethargic for a few months. I had a check up and they found nothing wrong with me. So I guess it's psychological.
AFB: How was your mood when your material worked?
Andy: I was up and away!
AFB: I get the impression that when it went well, you let your excitement over a female show. If that's true then it is very likely that you succeeded with women because of your show of lively interest in them.
Andy: When I feel like myself, I do get excited and happy when I meet an attractive woman. But the lines are important.

AFB: Why?
Andy: They make me feel more confident.
AFB: Why are they important now when they no longer work?
Andy: I want them to work again.
AFB: When your mood comes back up why not try approaching someone new with just the lively and happy interest she makes you feel. Why not put aside the lines and see what happens just by giving her your feelings.
Andy: What are you saying?
AFB: It's not the line that makes the connection. It's how you offer yourself and how much she can see what she does to you, in a good sense, in how you express yourself.
Andy: Lines and my material take time to get together. And I enjoy putting it all together.
AFB: That's good. But it's not what a female wants. If you prepare what you will say or do beforehand how is she going believe that what she sees then and there is what she is doing to you at that time? The preparation may make you feel better but it also cuts your spontaneity when you meet her, and she will notice it.
Andy: So I should give her the good feelings she gives me, when my mood is back up.
AFB: You can even do that now. There is no need to wait for your mood to lift. If some lovely lights your fire, then do what you just said, give her the good feelings she gives you. That's most of what women really want.
Andy: I need to sleep on this. I never thought of my material working because I was doing something else right. (pause) I think I need to try it myself and see. But the idea does make sense of what's happening to me now.

Myths: Lines and Ploys   241

Lines and ploys often have great comic value, especially when the conjuring up experience is shared by several males. The mirth and positive feeling that follow may be of great value in later giving women what they really want. If a female so impresses a male that he then goes and spends time dreaming up what to say or do, then he already feels the feelings that she so much wants to know she created in him. A next step to succeed with her is study what she does to you, and how to let it go to her in a natural way, rather than studying beforehand what to say or what action to take.

The idea of using a ruse or contrivance makes a strong appeal to the male tendency to take to action. The idea can also create feelings of confidence. Such activity, or preparation, away from her can serve a very good purpose if you give your attention more to why you want to dream up something than to dreaming it up. Taking action is a male way. Feeling emotions and finding them delicious is more a female way. When you are with her she will admire your capacity to take action but she will want to give you her affections if your feelings and expressions show her what good things she is stirring in you. If lines and ploys have a real value, it may be in bringing a male to see why he wants to use them and then to releasing the personal energy she really wants see. The energy she longs for is not in creating a tactic but in what she made him feel in the first place that would so drive him to create something. The closer you come to spontaneously expressing that first energy, the one that comes from what you see in her, the more certain you can be of success.

GUIDED EXERCISE. Feel the energy that counts! Recall a time when you wanted to use a line or ploy. Run your experience backwards with visualization till you arrive at that first energy, the energy she wants to see!

GUIDED ANSWER. Here is how this exercise went with Andy.

AFB: Begin by going back to a time when your material worked for you.
Andy: There is a honey of a female that I saw many times at the coffee shop at work. One day I decided I was going to connect with her. I began to think of my favorite lines. (pause)
AFB: This will work best if you play the whole thing in your imagination first, then go back to the very beginning.
Andy: OK. Give me a while to run it across my mind. (pause) OK, I'm back to where I am beginning to look at her in the coffee shop. I'm walking in and I see her where I expected to. My pulse goes up, my eyes go wide with how pretty she is and I feel my breath stop for her. She is so nice to look at! Not just her looks, but the way she moves and carries herself. I just know that she would be great to be with. (pause)
AFB: Keep going, Andy. Any images come to your mind just now?
Andy: I'm see myself dancing with her and feeling her silky, graceful way. I see myself in the park with her and picking a flower for her hair. I see her smile all over the place!
AFB: Good. Now try to find how to put those feelings into your lines with her.
Andy: I thought lines don't work very well.

AFB: It's the something else you express when you feel you must use a line that makes the interplay with her successful. It would help if you could see how to put all those good feelings into your lines with her.

Andy: OK. (pause) I can see that. As I approach her I am wearing the biggest smile because of all these thoughts of her and me. She sees my full smile and smiles back. She knows I'm going to say something and almost steps up to me to hear it. I said something like her phone number has to be better than mine. And she likes it!

AFB: She likes all the good energy you are giving her. The line is an afterthought.

Andy: Are you sure?

AFB: Imagine how your interaction would have gone if you said exactly the same thing but with a serious face and in a low key way.

Andy: That would never work.

AFB: So?

Andy: Let me think. (pause) Well, I can see that the bounce in my approach lit her up. Maybe I could have said just anything and that would have worked too.

AFB: That is very likely. She likes seeing how good she makes you feel, and then seeing those emotions come back to her. Your words are just the messenger, so to speak.

Andy: This could work! Let me think it over.

Chapter 22.

Older Men, Younger Women

Can't help lovin' that man of mine.

...from Oscar Hammerstein's Can't Help Loving That Man

Something very interesting happens in puberty between boys and girls. It's something that tends to stay in place in most of the world's cultures. Girls enter puberty earlier than boys, at least most of the time. A girl at this time is brimming with wonderful new feelings and powers, and wants to learn about them with boys of a like mind. Most boys her age have not entered puberty and so she must look to boys older than herself for mutual interest. Little of this changes in the later part of puberty.

A girl several years into puberty will not be likely to date boys at or near her own age because those boys will be some years behind her sexually. At this later point in puberty, or early adolescence, most girls have little choice but to date older boys in order to find comparable sexual and emotional maturity, not to mention interest and willingness. From the very beginning of their own sexual flowering females learn to look to men a little older than themselves for likely partners.

The young female's need to seek the company and affection of older males often evolves into a pattern for all of life. Adolescent females form their romantic hopes and wishes with the perception that older males have the maturity to satisfy them. When this begins, around puberty, females have little or no idea of the many kinds of growth and maturity that life will bring them. They have equally little idea of how life will later rework the boys they so much want to be with. The yen for the older male begins with a preference for males who are perhaps several years older than themselves and that yen stays in place in most women. The growth that comes with each next stage of life, in themselves and in men, has little effect on this preference.

As females mature they often note the many strengths of males who are more than just a few years older than themselves. The prospects of enjoying an older man's seasoning and life experience, and of making a deeper and more meaningful romantic tie with him, often turn women's eyes to men who are considerably older than they are. A woman who sees the prospect of emotional satisfaction with an older man will quickly ignore his age, even if she was put off by it at first. The age difference between a woman and the man who feels right for her can be anywhere from five to twenty years or even more.

There are a number of myths about older men and younger women. An amusing one is that older men are less sexually satisfying than younger men. This myth amuses by ignoring many facts. The older man usually knows much more than the younger man about how to make love to a woman in a way that both excites and pleases her. He usually knows more about the psychological part of foreplay and lovemaking itself. The easiest part of love making to learn is the mechanics and most men eagerly master this knowledge very early in their sexual life. It takes living and learning from one's shortfalls to get in touch with the emotional part of a woman's sexual wishes, and here the older man has a commanding lead.

Another interesting myth is that older men and younger women are at stages of life that are too different for their relationship to work. Older men usually have more ability to appreciate a younger woman than men near her age. There is little, if anything, a woman wants more earnestly than to be appreciated for what she is and for what she can bring to a relationship. This need is so deep, and the older man so attractive at this level, that most women won't see an older man but a better opportunity. It is near to an axiom that the more a male satisfies a woman emotionally, the less she sees anything but the satisfaction.

The adult stage of life is longer than any other. In this long period from the early twenties to well into the fifties and sometimes even much later, a male has many powers and capacities to enjoy. A younger female seeking love, affection, company, fun, family or some other personal gain, can fulfill her wishes with an adult male who is in this longest part of a lifetime. A woman with a first wish for a man near her in age will give up that wish upon finding an older man who offers her his richer personality and the life skills that time has given him. The span of adult life, the sustained powers and joys of this period and the wisdom and resourcefulness of the older, seasoned male are among the most ignored and least applied advantages that the older male has. And again, the female's deep hunger for a man to savor what she is gives the older man a formidable edge in the competition for her.

The availability of younger women and the older man's access to them is often a difficult point for men to accept or even to open themselves to. It is uncommon, in some places rare, for a male to choose an older female. This may make it difficult for a male to seriously think in terms of succeeding with a younger female because a man is likely to wonder, at one level or another, why a woman should fare better with an older lover than a man doing likewise. Some men still look back to the time of their puberty and the impressive lead that older females had on them, a thought that can make women who are younger than these men seem unprepared or callow. And some men simply can't imagine fortune being so kind as to deliver a younger woman for them to enjoy. Yet the option is there because younger women are taken with older men, including men that are many years older than themselves. The greater nearness of the female psyche to the personality itself and to emotional rewards is entirely in favor of the older male who has an eye for younger women and good feelings for them.

Another deep need in women is their longing to feel grounded. The male who can make her feel as though all her parts come together better by his presence is very much what a woman wants. A younger man, near her own age, will be better able to make light of her cares and even to enjoy her love of life when it goes silly. The older man, with his greater awareness of himself and her, will be more aware of her need to feel grounded and also more able to satisfy it. The older man is more able to support her with understanding and sweet affection as she gives herself to life, to him and to becoming more as a woman. This is one reason why women tend to see the older man as more giving. A good rule of thumb here is that younger women will look more to men near their own age for fun, and will look more to older men for joys and satisfactions in love and romance.

There are times when the coming together of an older man and a younger woman is just about inevitable. An older man who needs to take time out from life to have fun is very likely to seek the company of a much younger woman. Men who are recently out of long term and committed relationships are apt to feel this way. Having fun with no aim in mind but to enjoy life and find new options makes the frisky and devil may care ways of a much younger woman just what the doctor ordered. A younger woman seeing such a yen in an older man is attracted twice over, once because he sees how much fun she would be and second because of the savvy ways he offers as an older and more experienced man.

There are other life situations that can drive a man more strongly toward younger women than older. Another is the man who after working long and hard comes to realize that life promises much more than just the rewards of work. This kind of man can easily be overtaken by a driven need to see what else life has in store. His drive is similar to that of a very young man just out to discover the world. And who better to do that with than a younger female who has a like need and a soul full of eager energy for the adventure he has in mind!

At times the drive comes the other way, from a female seeking older men. Young females are easily excited by the energy and risk taking ways of young men near their own age. In time almost all females come up against their deep inner need to feel grounded, supported and emotionally understood. When this kind of frustration goes on long enough, a younger female is likely to seek the warmth and affection of an older male. A young woman with her heart torn between the vibrant energy of a young lover and the deep satisfactions and stability of the older man will most of the time choose the older man.

A major issue for older men finding options with younger women is the sense of entitlement to it. It is common for older men to admire the youth of a younger woman to the point of feeling disqualified from her life. This can be a missed opportunity because younger women admire older men and have more difficulty hiding their attraction to older than younger men. In fact, most women are more willing to let their attraction to an older man show than to a younger one. Too often the older man gives the bargain away by assuming not enough interest from the younger female, not seeing that he has more of a hold over her than vice versa. A younger female seeing this is not likely to feel that she has an advantage but that he has given up his. She will not be likely to pursue him because that works too much against the needs of her own nature. Most of the time she will choose to wish for him and pine away, hoping that he sees his advantage with her and acts on it.

These ideas come to most men as welcome surprises. It is remarkable how few older men see how seductive younger women find them. A well rounded man young in his mid-thirties felt drawn to a woman about ten years younger than himself. He wished to know how such a relation could work. Call him Jerry.

Jerry: This all began with a phone call. I had to contract out a piece of my own contract and had a bid that looked good. So I met with the subcontractor and she turned out to be one gorgeous, foxy lady. I know that she saw how she got to me. (pause) She's about ten years younger than I am but I don't care about that. I'm hoping she'll feel the same.
AFB: Has she shown interest in you?
Jerry: I'm not sure. She called a few times for things that weren't necessary. I'm not sure of myself here. Older men, younger women, hey they have all the marbles!
AFB: What if you pushed her buttons as much as she pushed yours?
Jerry: That didn't happen.
AFB: Pretend.
Jerry: Pretend?
AFB: Assume you get to her like she gets to you. Then what?
Jerry: Well, if that really happened she would be taking walks at night like me to try to figure how to get to me. That's a really nice idea! (pause) But how could such a thing work? A woman that attractive can have her choice anytime.

AFB: What if you are her choice?
Jerry: Why would that happen?
AFB: For starters, you selected her for your subcontract. She can't help feeling that you see value in her, even if it is just work. The way you talk about her suggests that she has good feelings for you and is probably waiting for you to do something.
Jerry: But if I did I would expect her to drop out anytime.
AFB: Why?
Jerry: She's that attractive.
AFB: What about you? Women think with their feelings. If you make her feel right with you, her monogamous way won't let her see anyone but you, for as long as you are good to her.
Jerry: I don't know about this.
AFB: Don't know about what?
Jerry: It just seems like she has all the trump cards.
AFB: Why must it be that only you are taken with her? Why can't she be even more taken with you? And aren't you suggesting that she would be fickle in a relationship?
Jerry: So you're saying that I'm counting myself out and giving her all the options. (pause) That may be true. Maybe if I tested her interest I would find that this isn't one way traffic after all.
AFB: You can show her your interest. She'll like that because she's a woman. Just be sure to also show her that you're not giving it all away, that she'll have to work to win you.
Jerry: Like I said, maybe this is true. I guess I'll have to feel her out and see if it is.

Now and then nature outdoes itself. This happens, for example, when a younger woman with a wish for an older man meets an older man with a wish for a younger woman. The older man gets high marks on all counts this time. His eyes for her rich youthful energy and zesty ways are just what she's looking for. And who better to savor all the glee in her offerings than a man who has seen enough to dish it up in large portions. His interest in her and his steady way tells her that she can count on him to be there for the things that are important to her. He promises her that wonderful sense of support that women of all ages long for. And she feels she can trust him to keep the good things coming because he is older and seasoned by life to good judgment and sensitivity. Here, as elsewhere, the major risk is in the man discounting how seductive he is to the younger woman and in treating her as though she has all the leverage because of the charms of her youth. The man who acts on his opportunity with the younger woman without discounting himself will soon find her working harder and harder for his interest and approval. This is true whether or not the female is as drawn to the male from the outset as vice versa.

GUIDED EXERCISE. Find a time when you wished to connect with a younger woman. Relive the event with an awareness of what she finds compelling about you.

GUIDED ANSWER. "I am sitting in a local shop and then I realize that a pretty woman, at least a dozen years younger than myself, is looking at me. This isn't the first time. I had seen her here before and her leggy look and fine features caught my eye. She's getting on line and now and then she looks back at me when she thinks I'm not looking at her. I know why I find her attractive but I wonder what pleases her about me.

"Her eyes and her long look tell me a story. She looks wistfully at me, like she's curious about me and really wants to get to know me. She gives me a steady look, different from how she looks at men her own age. This makes me feel that she's imagining what I would be like as compared to a younger man. I think to myself that she likes how much more I know about life and how to enjoy it than younger men and maybe herself. Her eyes come at me with affection, almost as if she knew me already. She must sense that I could really find her inviting and that I enjoy being good to a woman I care about.

"Her look makes me feel like she sees a better way with me than with men her own age. She makes me feel that I could get closer to her than they could and she would like that — so would I! Her sweet, easy ways get to me and I think my steady ways get to her."

Chapter 23.

More Myths: The Handsome Man, Wealth and Power

Tell the boys I've got the Luck with me now.

...from The Luck of Roaring Camp by Bret Harte

Some men are so gifted with personal beauty that they do to women what beautiful women do to men. Women throw themselves at such men and abandon all thoughts of being coy and all concerns about compromising themselves. However, women do not throw themselves at men the way men throw themselves at women. A female wanting an option with a handsome man will begin by adoring, even worshipping, his beauty. She does this with little thought of action, the way a male would. She takes in the magnificent view and lets it go to work on her because she loves the way it makes her feel. She hopes to get to know him, in a passing way, because she feels that his remarkable beauty must somehow be related to her own.

She finds her enchantment with his male way increased by how his beauty presents it. One part of him, his male energy, draws her on because it gives her something she cannot fully give herself. Another part, his remarkable beauty, captivates her by its likeness to something about herself. A man with such immense attractive power for a woman reminds her at once of what she does to men. A woman then feels that she must admire the handsome man because, in a certain way, he has the same seductive power as herself. A woman knows that she is one of nature's great works of art and how this goes to work on men. She finds the man with the astonishingly good looks an exciting joy to behold and, soon after, she finds that she must admire him as a peer to her own powers, but in the other gender. Ultimately she feels that he is an opportunity to see live and close up what she does to men by studying what he does to her. This is one of many reasons why women tend to respect and admire the handsome man.

The head turning male creates some self indulgent wishes in a female. Women manage this differently from men who come upon a beautiful woman. Her wish is not to get to know him in any deep sense of the idea or to date him or to have a relationship. Her wish is usually to get close to this marvel of nature for a brief time, to enjoy him and to get more of a sense of what beauty in a male is about and how, if at all, it differs from her own. She will feel this way even if he is otherwise disappointing in large ways. Her enjoyment may only be her close up look at him with a chance for some conversation. Sometimes the enjoyment goes further, at times much further, but the outcome tends to be the same. Most of the time the outcome is also different from what other men, who may see this happen, are likely to assume.

The Handsome Man, Wealth and Power 257

I once saw this played out in a striking way. I was in an auto showroom and the salesman I spoke with was certainly one of the most handsome men I had ever seen. He was in his twenties with black hair, deep and bright blue eyes, a completely handsome face and an athletic physique too. Another salesman began to chat with me and we fell into conversation about the handsome one because I thought I had seen him in soap operas. The one who was speaking suggested that I watch what happens when a female comes in. I took his advice. A female entered, looked at the latest model cars and spoke with a salesperson until she saw the handsome fellow. Then everything changed. She lost interest in everything but his remarkable looks. She immediately sought him out to speak to and to get a better look at him. Her rapture with his beauty could not be more obvious. And if he wanted her phone number it would have been very easy for him to get it. This scenario repeated several times as other females came in and caught sight of him. They simply adored him. They had to be close to his beauty and do honor to it. And that's as far as it went. None of the women showed any sign of interest in the handsome man that went past enjoying him as a work of art or perhaps as a passing tryst.

Women are governed by very stable and deep inner longings. A woman, as much or more than a man, can be spellbound by beauty but that changes nothing in her inner self and her needs. If the handsome man does not satisfy her basic needs then the magic of his beauty will count for little and she will soon be on her way. Women can only want what their natures hunger for. Remarkably good looks are not a high priority with the vast majority of women, perhaps nearly all of them. Emotional sensitivity and a genuine interest in their make up is a very high priority with women. If the man who pleases her is also handsome then that is good. However a man of mediocre looks who satisfies her emotional make up will instantly move to the front of the line past the handsome one, and this is also true of men who have poor looks.

A woman may well take her pleasure with a handsome man. When she does she will usually feel that she is sporting with the other gender the way that men do with women. She will even feel entitled to do what men do. Women share a collective myth that men exploit them, especially the most beautiful ones. When a woman has a brief encounter with a handsome man her joy and interest are sincere. So are her wishes to do good works for her gender. Side by side with the honest thrill and excitement of being with a man so well formed are emotions that belong to her sister females. Those emotions want women to take the rights and privileges that men take with women, according to their (the women's) myth. How much the myth agrees with reality counts for little. It is the belief that men have far more liberties with women than vice versa that creates the feeling of a victory for her gender.

The aftermath is a good memory that will easily bring her a smile. That handsome man quickly becomes a memory and rarely becomes more. Her time with him makes her even more aware of what she really wants in a lover. Her heart is in her emotional need to be close to a man who has affection for her worth and the pleasing differences of her nature. The man who does that is her prince and he is more handsome to her than any other. The man who does that makes her feel that nothing could be more natural or fitting than to give him her love, her sweet affection and her soulful ways. This is real luck for a male and forms the intended meaning of the quote from Bret Harte at the beginning of this chapter. Any man can create this kind of luck by giving a woman what she really wants, regardless of how far from handsome he may be. And what she really wants is what you already are, with an openly expressed interest in her.

Many women have a first attraction to men who are wealthier than themselves. This interest comes from a healthy and wholesome part of a woman's nature and differs from what men may first think of it. For themselves, men usually see money as a thing that creates liberty and options. Women enjoy that part of money too but their greatest pleasure in money is found elsewhere. Money appeals to a woman's need to feel grounded, a need that is much stronger in a female than a male. Grounding means that she has some security that her emotions will stay in place and not run off on their own, and that she is safe from certain unpleasant feelings such as isolation and helplessness. A woman responds to money this way because it makes her feel that she has some of the male strengths and ways nature gave her less of. In other words, some of her reaction to money is the same as her reaction to a caring man. Her feelings about money are a cousin of the male's because money gives her options on how to feel more grounded, freer and less concerned about emotional cares. At bottom, women unconsciously equate money with the male power they wish to enjoy with a lover, because a loving male freely offers his strength to her wish for it.

One myth about women and money is that women want to be regaled and set on a pedestal. Women do want men to treat them in a special way early on, but once she comes to care this takes a back seat to her wish to give and get loving and romantic feelings. This is even true of women for whom money is a goal in itself for these women put off satisfying their emotional wishes until they can rest easy about finances. There is a kernel of truth in the myth that women want money to be free of care. As noted, women want to be at ease about their ongoing concern with feeling grounded. As for those loathsome cares that make life run, women are usually better at managing details than men. In fact, most women actually enjoy the details. Their concern is not to be carefree in a male sense, but to be more able to happily manage life by first feeling centered and grounded. This means that money puts to rest a different concern in women than in men.

A woman would rather have a man's way dispel her concern than have more money, but the first lure of money remains something for her to work through in a relationship. She can no more easily turn away from the hope of feeling more in possession of herself via money than she can turn away from a man who feels right for her. Most women are aware of this issue and they go from gratitude to love with the man who offers his way to her need. A woman is also grateful when the man she cares about understands how much this concern pulls at her. She then gives more and more of herself to this man because his understanding is part of the becoming one with her nature that she so much wants. And she well knows that his way is much better than money could ever be.

As noted, wealth in a man makes a first appeal to a specific female need and women want to give their affection to the man who satisfies that need. Her satisfaction does not depend upon money. The wealthy male who does not satisfy her emotionally will soon find himself alone because money by itself does not create enough positive emotions to make a woman feel satisfied. She wants a man who can show her the good and happy things she does to him and who can send his directed male way to her. Again, women very much prefer the male who makes them feel grounded with his male ways over money. A woman looks at a man with emotional eyes that want to satisfy his and her own needs in a relationship. A man's wealth does not rival his offering her the good feelings she wants and needs in a relationship. She takes the male who makes this preferred offering to mean that he has discovered her because a male must see the way of her nature to satisfy it. She then regards the male who makes her feel right as wise and deserving her best gifts.

A man whose position in life and the world gives him power has some of the same effect on women as men who are wealthier than the women they meet. A woman sees the excitement of male mastery in the man whose words and will can change the world around him. The exaggeration of male ways in the man of power floods a woman with positive emotions that can spellbind her and carry her away. The idea of having such power in her life to meet certain of her emotional needs comes to her like a dreamed of wish fulfillment. A woman revels in the images that a man of power creates in her and feels that her wishes for romance and stability can be satisfied with him. Many men in many ages have commented on this aphrodisiac effect of male power on women. Its greatest meaning is not to learn how to acquire power but to learn how to give her the part of you that gives a woman the feelings and mood she so much wants.

Like money, power offers a woman a means to feel grounded and to feel free of concern about how her thoughts and feelings may leave each other or how she might otherwise become undone. All men have the power to make a woman feel more fulfilled and more like the serene master of herself. A female's adoration of male power comes from what it does to her inner self, unlike a male's admiration that usually goes to what power can do in life and the world. Women are thrilled, at least for a while, by male power for a number of reasons. One is her anticipation of how that power will go to work on her. Other reasons come from how power is put to use, that is, aggression. That last word — aggression — is used here in the healthy sense of mastery and not the unhealthy sense of hostility.

Where there's power, aggression is not far off. And where there's aggression, sexuality is not far off either. Human nature is hard pressed to feel the one without also feeling the other, a point made in chapter 18. This makes power something of an aphrodisiac in a literal sense. Power offered to a female by a male with a good regard for himself has a delicious feeling of mastery that women hunger for. Its first appeal, again, is to ground and center a woman, and its appeal to sexual excitement follows closely after. Her sexual arousal over power and aggression is not an end in itself. It is the beginning of many feelings and hopes rooted in herself as a life giver, and the last phrase — life giver — is the truest meaning of sex to her.

A woman is quick to assume that her own ideals on the use of power are alive and well in the powerful man she meets. The female instincts to create, nurture and support life are near the surface. These things make women ready to notice a man of power because of their hope that he will use it in a worthwhile way with her. This expectation, or hope, makes the man of power even more seductive to her, at first. Her awareness of her life giving powers seeks out his power as a thing that she wants to have to safeguard and care about life. This very old instinct in the female is one of many reasons why females so admire males of good intention. Women see such men as in line with their own nature and purpose. They also see proof in such men against abuse of power, a thing they deeply fear.

A man of power who does not offer his power to a woman's wishes will soon find himself looking for someone new. A woman will take a man of modest means who shows her what good things she does to him and who sends his purposeful male way to her over a powerful man. The lure of power is rarely in a female wish to be powerful, but in what new and good things male power makes her feel and experience. The man who is powerful in life or the world is a large reminder to women of what they hope the power of a male will do to them. The male whose natural power goes to her hopes for what it does to her wins her love and affection, whatever his financial worth or his status in the world.

A man of great means struggled with how his worth and position got him no further than the beginning of love relationships. His core issue was weak empathy. Call him Glen.

Glen: People who hear me talk of wanting to find someone tell me money is not everything. I'm not even looking for a wealthy woman, I'm looking for love and romance. I'm not concerned about success at the first meeting with her. That usually goes very well. It's getting to second base that's become an issue.
AFB: Do you have any thoughts about getting to second base?
Glen: I treat a woman very nicely when I first meet her. I try to show her that I have good things in mind for the two us by wining and dining her. No problem with that part. I remain generous as things move along and then they slowly lose interest.
AFB: Do you lose interest too?
Glen: No, I just withdraw when I see them fizzling out.
AFB: Suppose you were with a female you liked and she did not fizzle out. How would things look then?
Glen: I would enjoy her company and treat her well. We would travel and find some adventure. We would do things, all kinds of things. Of course, I would enjoy her affection.
AFB: Have you suggested doing this with any one of them?
Glen: Sure, when things have gone on for more than about a month or so, I like to bring it up. (pause)
AFB: And?

The Handsome Man, Wealth and Power 265

Glen: And what?
AFB: And how does she receive it?
Glen: It usually amounts to I'll think about it. When things come to this point I usually feel like she wants something and she's not telling me.
AFB: That sounds right.
Glen: How could you know?
AFB: You speak with good interest in women but if I were a woman I would feel that you see one part of me and not the rest.
Glen: Is this about sex?
AFB: No. The part you see is a woman as an affectionate companion.
Glen: And the other part?
AFB: Women want to see that you see their emotions and find them interesting, energizing and important to both of you.
Glen: Well, if I want to share some adventure with her why am I not doing that?
AFB: It's not what you do with her but how you do it. Picking up on her feelings, enjoying them and seeing them as special is something you can do anywhere, anytime. Women can never really get enough of it.
Glen: So my wealth is making for a good first connection, but I need to get more of a sense of a woman as a female?
AFB: It's more than your wealth. You really are interested in women and they sense that and like it. A woman is likely to assume that your interest will keep going to other parts of her. In time she probably feels that you are not getting the message.
Glen: The message from her personality or emotions. Is that it?
AFB: That's what it sounds like.
Glen: Is this something I can learn?

AFB: Sure, there are many things you can do to open up your sensitivity. If a woman you're dating knows about your efforts she will admire you and want to help you with it.
Glen: Really?
AFB: Really.
Glen: I think I should get to work on this. (pause) But first let me think it over and make sure it makes sense.

It would be wonderful to have some or all of good looks, wealth and power and to also have the intimate connection with her emotions and personality that a woman wants. Without doubt, this would be an unrivalled mix. Fortunately, women rate your seeing their beauty and emotional merits and giving her your joy over these things in your expressions above all else. This is no more than normal empathy with a little more of self expression than most males give to women. None of the above three advantages for a first meeting — good looks, wealth or power — can compete with the man who makes the offering that connects with a woman's nature and shows happiness over it. The male who learns to do this a little better than average already rivals any of these three advantages in a first meeting with a female he favors. And the same is true of later meetings with her.

GUIDED EXERCISE. Women want you to be presentable and to have enough, not to be handsome or rich or powerful. Relive a successful flirtation and find the moments where you knew you were succeeding. Study those moments for what of your good looks, worth or power play a part, then look for why it really went well.

GUIDED ANSWER. "There's a pretty lady who comes to visit her girl friend in my building. She's too attractive to pass by so I flirted with her in the elevator. As we got on I smiled at her and she smiled back. I could see she knew I wanted to get to know her. She seemed to give me an opening by giving me her floor number to press when I was closer to the buttons than she was. I pressed many buttons before her floor so that the elevator would stop and give me time. We made small talk about her being from out of town and when she finally noticed the elevator stopping with no one getting on or off I broke out laughing. She gave me a knowing look and began to laugh too. I knew I was getting to her at this point.

"When we got to her floor I got out with her and then walked with her. She commented on the coincidence that I lived on the same floor as her friend. I told her that I lived on another floor and again broke out laughing. She liked that. I could see my interest in her was welcome. I said that if she knew when she was leaving I would meet her in the lobby for coffee and conversation. When she hesitated I said I would play the elevator game every time she visited until she agreed, and then she agreed with a large and sweet grin.

"This worked well. She could see at once that I am not handsome, though I'm not bad looking either. Anybody living where I lived would have to be middle class, and I am. As for power, she knows that I'm an illustrator. I know why this worked. She struck a note in me and I really enjoyed flirting with her. I was open, playful and direct, and she loved it!"

PART IV
MAKING IT HAPPEN

Part IV has two final chapters. They are about how to put all the success material together for the best use at getting the love and romance that you want. There are no exercises and no dialogues from success coaching in these last chapters. From here on life is your best exercise and, as you move toward it, no other man's dialogues can speak for how you are to grow the art of success.

Part IV spells out the principles that will lead you to the art of succeeding with women. It also describes the attitude that enables you to get the most from the principles. You will get the most from your efforts if you work at the principles and the optimal attitude at the same time. Doing so will both energize you and shorten the distance to the success you want.

Chapter 24.

The Art of Success

Success depends on three things: who says it, what he says, how he says it; and of these three things, what he says is the least important.

...from Recollections, by John, Viscount Morley of Blackburn

The art of succeeding with women, like every art, grows as you master its basic principles. As you learn how to apply them you will create more of the success you want and get more out of life. The principles are given in the first three parts of this book, with emphasis on the meaning that counts, their emotional meaning. The first part presents basics to help you begin to experience the ways that work and to grow them for your use and enjoyment. The second part goes more deeply into the nature of the winning ways and how to grow them more, especially by finding that they were in you all along. On the surface, the third part is about special issues. It is really an application of the basic principles to show that what is usually taken for a problem, such as being a shy or intellectual man, is actually an advantage when properly managed. The material now comes to a point for explicitly stating what the principles are and describing how they come together to create the success you want.

The material quoted at the beginning of this chapter emphasizes that success depends on how you offer what you have to say, rather than on what you say. This means that your delivery is a major key to success. This is a point whose mastery will bring you great rewards and it is well worth your best attention. The three ideas cited in the quoted material are true of every successful venture involving other people. They are true in a general sense, but more is needed in order to succeed with women. It happens that the number of principles for succeeding with women is also three. They reveal how to express the delivery that works, at first meetings with the women you wish for and later.

The discovery principle, mentioned earlier a number of times, comes first. It makes a woman want to be with you the moment she feels what it does to her. It makes her immediately long for more of you because you do to her what she hoped for before she met you. The discovery principle is about a very deep need in a woman when it comes to men. It is about a feeling and fulfillment that she values very highly for all the joy and pleasure it gives her. It makes her see only you because she believes that if you did this to her once, and early on, you can do it to her over and over again. It is called the discovery principle because of its emotional meaning to a woman and because of how it takes place. Nothing rivals this principle in its importance to your success or its importance to women.

Here is a scenario that portrays what the discovery principle is and what need in a female it satisfies. There is a female whom you see and with whom you want to connect. Before she meets you she is hoping for a male who will see her worth and be excited over it and made happy by it. She sees her worth in the rich feelings that she wishes to lovingly give to a male, as well as in the rich feelings she gives herself. Her worth is her silky and intuitive way that greets a male and tells him that she is wonderful to be with. Her worth is in what happiness her lines, her feelings and overall beauty can give you. She longs for a male who will see her many kinds of goodness and merit, become excited and joyful over it, and then show her what she does to him with his welcome emotions.

She muses on these hopes before a next male enters her life. Many come and go and leave her wanting because they do not have eyes for enough of her. This makes her feel that an uncommon man, a man who is special and perhaps wise, will come along and find her. Such a man makes her feel that at last he is discovering her value when so many others see too little of all the magical things she is as a female. She wants to share what she has and is with a male who sees it and who gives her the happiness he finds with her in the obvious way of his expressed emotions. She knows that she cannot stop her spirit and affections from leaping out to the male who gives her this most treasured of all satisfactions that she can have as a lover.

The male in the scenario is up to enough self expression to make her feel what he feels. This means that he is spontaneous enough and has a high enough regard for himself and his make up to freely express what she does to him. His natural way with his own feelings makes it easy for her to read them and to feel them herself. This is a soul satisfying experience for her and she will never stop wanting more of it because it is the main event in her love life. She opens to him more and more upon seeing his welcome delight with her. This makes his energy and enthusiasm for her grow and they quickly begin to feed off of each other. The more he shows that he is finding her and the good in her the more she gives him to revel in. He cannot withhold his delight and she cannot keep from giving him to more delight in. His welcome and her offer move more and more quickly to each other and soon she feels that she has finally come upon him, the one who knows how to find happiness in what she is, what she can offer and what she can be with him.

This scenario is about more than just appreciating a woman. The discovery principle is about actually seeing the wonders of a woman and wanting them because you also see what happiness, joy and goodness they bring. It is very much a matter of giving to her your first happy emotional response to what you really see in her. This is why the shy man has an edge. A woman sees immediately that his shyness is telling her that he is seeing her worth as a woman and as a lover. His shyness tells her how much he wants what he sees because it is so good that he must pause. No woman can turn from eager male eyes upon her, eyes that see and want her person, her lines, her seductive ways and the glee of her spirit. A woman's response to seeing a male discover her fills her with a very strong desire for him, and for more of what he does to her. A woman feels fulfilled and as if her love life is on purpose with the male who does this to her. She looks upon what he does as a great gift that she must have and which she will eagerly purchase with her affections and admiration, for a woman must admire the man who finds her in this sense.

This need is so basic and its fulfillment so rich in pleasure that a woman will not turn to a second male who also appears to be discovering her after a first one does so. She knows with certainty what the first one does to her and she also knows how long she has waited for this to happen. Her need is so great and her emotions of joy and gratitude toward the first one so powerful that she will not risk the certainty of the first on a gamble that yet another male can do this to her.

A woman's emotions become so energized by the male who sees her and wants what he sees that she will forego almost anything for the sake of what he does to her. Her need is so deep and her satisfaction so rich that she will give almost anything to have the man who does this to her as her very own. The history of love and romance tells on this. Many men through the ages, mostly gigolos who had an intuition for the discovery principle, received fortunes from the women that they so gratified. Women of means spared no expense to have these men who loved them as they wished to be loved in their lives. The point is not to advocate for the gigolo but rather that this need is so important to women that they will only see and want the man who satisfies it. How could it be otherwise when this man gives her what she spends most of her time wishing and hoping for?

There are many ways to express that you are finding, that is, discovering her. From among them all playfulness is one of the healthiest and most fun loving ways to do so. A woman knows intuitively that when a man plays with her he is expressing images of already being with her. She takes this to mean that he sees what good things lie ahead in a relation with her. His high spirits and lively way tell her that he is already enjoying her. Playfulness comes on its own, most of the time, from seeing the joy, fun and many good things that will come from getting to know her and being with her. This means that it is natural to go from a smile for her to playing with her as you sense how much she would add to your life.

Most cultures of the world favor natural and open expression of emotion more in females than in males. Many cultures are simply opposed to such expression in males. This is a way of life from a remote time. It comes from the early part of human history where the male's greater strength was needed for hunting and building, and the female's tender intuitions went to children, family and tribe or community. Those times are gone and a male will profit immensely by looking at how much there is to gain, in succeeding with women and elsewhere, by opening up to natural and spontaneous expression of his feelings. This leads to the welcome bottom line that the man who freely express what a woman he likes does to him will win her time after time.

The road to mastering the discovery principle leads to far more success with women and to a richer and happier experience of yourself. There is an uphill grade for most men on this road to greater rewards.

That grade is in moving away from the time honored way of the male who expresses his feelings too little and toward an easier and more natural style of letting his feelings tell their own story. The man who does this will spontaneously give a woman what makes for success because what she really wants is to see the good things she does to him, spoken in the language of his feelings. This is another way of stating what the discovery principle really means, as well as how to live and enjoy it.

There are two parts to mastering this principle whose benefits reach far and wide in your life. The easier one is learning to watch your feelings and what they mean. Most males have some sense of this to begin with and most of the challenge is to get better at it. One good way to get started is to pay more attention to your female friends, relatives and acquaintances. Females set a good example and it is usually easy to watch them picking up on their feelings. It pays to talk with and watch females as they find your meanings in how you make them feel. Movies, lively conversation, art and reading all help here.

The second part is about opening more to self expression, especially of your emotions and moods. This is best done by letting yourself be attracted to good feelings in other people and life in general. It helps to seek things that make you want to feel good, such as having fun, laughing, eating and so on. The idea is to do something that easily creates a good feeling that seeks its own expression and then to add more to how you release it. The company of females helps here too. You can watch them do it first or, better, you can share with a female what you are trying to do. She will respect and admire you for doing what her nature does more easily and she will be eager to help you. In fact, she will think you are wise for studying what is more natural to her, an important point already made a number of times. Be careful about which female you choose for this because she will find this kind of ambition in you to be seductive; learning from her implies that you already have discovered some of her and the latter will excite her.

The last step before live practice with women you want to be with is dress rehearsal. This involves visualizing the woman you wish to connect with, going through the steps with your imagination and watching your feelings and emotions enter what you do. Welcome them, find out what they mean and express them as freely as you can. Some typical meanings will be pleasure, anticipation, excitement, hope and determination. Let any words at all come to mind to express what your feelings say and speak them to the image that created them. Do this several times a day for at least five minutes each time, preferably fifteen, and watch your gains accumulate. You will soon enjoy watching your freer and richer expressions create more first successes, and enjoyment, for you. This usually happens after one to two weeks of practice.

Some men say that classes in dance, acting and music have helped a great deal at this point. It also helps to seek out friends who express themselves this way because you will unconsciously learn their ways and begin to live them yourself. People who reply to others effortlessly, and with relish, are likely to be good examples of how feelings want to be their own message. There is also much to be gained by giving more expression to all the parts of your life. If you do that then you will more quickly master the art of succeeding with women and also improve many other, possibly all, parts of your life.

One more time because of its great importance to success, the discovery principle is about the good feelings and happiness that a female gives you and then showing her what she does to you. It is the single largest part of the art of succeeding with women. This principle comes from how women wish to be energized by the feelings you return to them. The next most important principle comes from how women wish to see men and how much they like to share their own experience. Women like to work together with others on what they need or what interests them. They are quick to strike up conversations with other women to create a welcome feeling of support in what they do. Women, who give so much support to those they care for, also wish to be supported at least as much. This is easy to see in how many men versus women come to socials by themselves, while women usually come with a group of their female friends.

When it comes to a lover the support she most wants is for your male energy to make her feel that all of her comes together and stays together, that is once again, to feel centered and grounded. She also wants your support and presence in the things that are important to her. This time it includes more than her feelings, for there are some things other than emotions that are very much female and not especially male. A woman quickly admires and wants more of a man who offers his help in the things that are important to her. It could be very ordinary such as helping her to match colors while decorating, helping her touch up furniture she cherishes, or helping her study for an examination. The way that counts is to support her purpose and that is the name of the second principle. Men who follow it do more than please her, they go to a high ranking among males in her eyes because women do not expect men to be cooperative and supportive this way. She will see the man who does this as acting on her wish to both find and share support, and she will feel drawn to him.

As noted several times, one of a woman's largest purposes is to feel grounded and for this she looks to men. She expects her lover to give her that good feeling and she is eager to reward him with things he cannot give himself. She wants but does not expect her lover to move with her in the other things she finds important. This is why her grateful affection, and respect, go to the man who supports her purpose. Women also see a man who does this as discovering her and choosing to be there for her.

Her intuition is that you cannot support her purpose if you do not know her, and you cannot know her well enough unless you discover her. Learning to support her purpose happens as you make gains with the discovery principle. The latter begins with those delectable feelings she creates in you by what she is and the latter then moves on to giving them to her. As you grow the art of expressing what she does to you, you will find it easier and more natural to sense more and more of her. Your affection and caring will move by themselves to these other parts of her as you come to see them and as your good feelings for her grow. In time areas that were not at first obvious will come into easy view. For example, when you first meet it is a matter of courtesy to help her with doors and obstacles but how could you know that the one you just met loves a man who can savor quiet moments together? Every little way you offer your energy to her purpose deepens her feeling that you are with her, and that makes her want to be with you more and more. And every such little offering also makes her feel more grounded, a deeply satisfying inner sense that can only make her want to get more of you, and to reward you!

Like the wish to feel grounded, the wish for you to support her purpose is part of her nature. Men really are bigger and stronger than women and better at directed, focused activity than women. A female's co-operative way wants to become one with your male strengths and to feel they are there for her. She feels grateful for your caring offers and loves how seductive she finds them. Women long for men whose ways create in them the kind of good feelings that they can only follow, and seek more of. Seduction has its healthy place in life and at its heart is creating her desire to be with you. Women want to be seduced in ways that agree with their nature, and here supporting her purpose goes a long and healthy way.

One of the least discussed forms of supporting her purpose is foreplay. Women want men to slowly wake them up sexually when making love. They cannot do this by themselves, except in an unsatisfying way, and they usually feel that the way you tenderly arouse them is also the way you will otherwise be with what is important to them. Foreplay begins before making love. In fact it begins when you first meet her. It's in the excited welcome you give her for her beauty, her sweet and uplifting ways, and her seductiveness. When you offer this to her with a wholesome feeling for it all she will have images of making love to you, but she is not likely to tell you until you get to know each other.

When a male acts on the first two principles, discovery and support, he satisfies a woman so much that she feels she must turn to him for more. This leads to the final principle of succeeding with women, trust. Regrettably the word trust usually brings to mind dark material on fidelity and monogamy. That's not what it means here! As for what it is not about, fidelity and monogamy, most women are content to remain unaware of what they don't know as long as you are satisfying them. Their liberal position on this usually comes from their belief that most men are governed by uncontrollable sexual drives to which they cannot say no.

The principle of trust is related to the good things you do to her when you fulfill the principles of discovery and support. Trust is least among the success principles and nowhere near the importance of discovery. However, the meaning of trust tells a great deal about how women see men and what men do to them. This understanding makes it easier to give both discovery and support to the female that interests you. There is a part of a woman's nature that is conservative. It is related to her biology as a life giver. Her intuition and instincts are ready to be there in large ways for those she loves, whether her lover or a family. She knows how important constancy is to loving and caring for others. When it comes to her being loved, she hopes for and very much values constancy from her lover. She finds great happiness in feeling that her lover will go on loving her and she finds doubts about this very unsettling. Again, the issue here is not about fidelity and monogamy.

The principle of trust means that a woman wants to feel sure that you will go on wanting her and doing to her the good things that you have been doing. This is almost entirely about her emotions and little of it has to do with possessions or money. This is one root of why most women are so liberal about the usual meaning of trust. When their emotional longings are fulfilled they do not care to trouble themselves about what else is going on as long as they feel certain that you will continue to light up their lives with what you do to them.

The principle of trust is also related to her need to feel grounded. When doubt enters a woman she loses some of that soul satisfying feeling of being one with her lover. Soon after she no longer has the feeling of being one with herself and with that she loses some of her sense of grounding. This troubles women, but on the plus side, it reveals why women have an admiration all their own for men who are honest and constructive. Women see integrity and good intention in such men as a promise or guarantee that they can keep turning to that kind of man for the happiness of love, affection and personal connection. Trust puts a woman's heart at ease and makes her eager and single minded about giving at least as much happiness to the man she loves as she receives from him.

These three principles, in their present form, are the result of recent research but they were known throughout the ages to artistically gifted people such as authors, poets and playwrights. These creative people enjoyed an immediate sense of how nature works and could see things in an easier and more intuitive way than most others. These special people put their wisdom into exquisite works of art that can make you experience their meaning. They have also left a larger lesson than just what they wrote or created. They found their understanding by opening to their own gifts and letting them go their own way, a thing you can do too. All three principles, and especially that of discovery, happen easily and by themselves when you let what that beguiling female does to you talk with its own voice. One of nature's most amazing gifts to living well is the success and happiness that comes by letting your nature go out to life on its own. The more you let life invite you and energize your expressions, the more you will live these three principles and succeed. This means that the more spontaneous you become, the nearer you come to the easy ways of the gifted of all ages who saw these principles in their own way, and who succeeded regularly with women, and often elsewhere.

These things are true in the other direction too. The way of nature is for women to easily flow to you with all the good they offer. The major difference, one of the few gender differences that are really there, is that women do this much more easily than men.

It is a given to a female that the male she cares about will attract her feelings with no further effort on her part. It is also a given that any male can make her feel centered and grounded and this is a given worth repeating. This helps answer a frequently asked question on the principles by men who feel all the work is on their side. Such men ask why is there not something that flows as effortlessly from men to women. The answer is that such a thing exists, and it is also the way of nature, but it is not the way most men are taught to live.

As noted, any male can thrill a female with the centering power of his way simply because he has what is common to all males. Any male by the same token can make her feel grounded. If any male can do these things then women must weigh other good things to make a choice among the males who want her. The largest difference between the man who succeeds and the one who doesn't is that the first is freer with himself as well as more accepting of himself. Such a man lets the good feelings she gives him flow back to her, on their own. Women know that this is an uncommon male trait and they value it very highly when they find it. This is why they are ready to see and quickly welcome such a male when he happens by.

It is the nature of things for men to do better than women at keeping unfit emotions at bay while thinking and taking action. When a male has no need to hold his feelings at arm's length it is nature's way for them to easily and spontaneously flow out of him. This is a larger and richer event in females than males and this is one reason why women read emotions so much more easily than men. The male view that he must do most of the work is matched by the female view that she has to bear so much frustration when it comes to getting his feelings or to getting him to sense her own. Both views point to the same thing, that men become happier and do better when they learn to let their feelings go out to those who stir them in the first place. A woman's immense beauty and goodness create welcome emotions of great energy in a man and she wants her return in kind from his expressions of them to her.

There are different ideas in the three principles of succeeding with women, but mastery of all three wants the action of your personality giving back to her what she does to you. This is easiest to see with the most important principle, discovery, where the good she does to you returns to her and makes her feel that you see her and like what you see. In flirting, affection and love a male's emotions are a far better messenger than his words. Your emotions also carry your message to her with a sparkling energy that thrills her and makes her want to move toward you.

Chapter 25

Position Yourself for Success

Nothing succeeds like success.

...from Ange Pitou by Alexandre Dumas the Elder

There is such a thing as a success attitude. It is a way to approach the art of success that brings the art to you faster and with more of the returns you want. It also adds more fun to the process and creates energy for it. Learning that attitude means that you will be able to review your results and quickly see how to go to a next level where you will do better. This is self coaching and it has points in common with how a coach prepares an athlete to perform better. Athletes are taught early on that their skill alone is not enough, but the way they regard the game can make for very large differences in outcome. The same is true with success in love and romance. There is a certain attitude, or form of regard, that will enable you to get the most from working with the success principles and to enjoy your adventure so much more.

The first impulse of the male way when presented with a wish is to seek the action that will make the wish come true. This is a great positive that helps males do large and satisfying things in work and other parts of life. When the goal is a woman's affections the male way can stall because of the mismatch between how a male makes his offering and how a female wants to receive it. This tends to repeat with most men and can, at times, be quite frustrating and discouraging. Positioning yourself for success means knowing how to use what is happening and not yet quite right to make it right. This part of a success attitude is about what you do from moment to moment when reaching for the good feelings of the woman whose affections you want.

Men are generally quick to take to action, and they are equally quick to sense that something more is needed when their sustained efforts do not produce as much as they want. This can easily happen, for example, when male actions try to speak to female emotions, or vice versa. There is no time at the moment of your interaction with the lovely female who interests you to sort things out. Your wish for her and for more of the art of success will both prosper if you keep on going. There are a few meanings in this at the same time.

For one, learn to accept the importance to success of continuing your pursuit even though you are uncomfortable and even though you do not yet understand what is happening. Continue to offer her your delight over being with her and let the other part of you, where you are uncomfortable or uncertain, simply be. This is more than the practical idea of not being distracted by feelings that are not entirely with you. Learning an art requires that you act before you feel ready and keep on going past the early efforts and the inevitable near misses. Accepting that you do not yet see all that is happening and even do not like how some of it feels is a large part of getting to the level of art or skill that brings you the consistent success you want.

This part of a success attitude is often called opening to unconscious learning. When you keep reaching for that special lady you want over and above discomfort and lack of insight, another part of you joins your effort. That other part is activated by your commitment to what you are doing. A deep and highly perceptive part of your personality works with you and for you behind the scenes at the moment of action and afterwards, as you make sense of what went well or otherwise. The male who keeps trying, who keeps rising above feelings that would rather make him leave, is the male who will unconsciously learn the meanings he wants and needs for success. This means that part of the wisdom in the idea that practice makes perfect is that who persists will unconsciously learn what works. And your inner understanding will become conscious as your skill grows and brings you more satisfaction.

Another meaning of staying on course, though it does not feel entirely right, is in the discovery principle. That lovely lady will sense that you are rising to the occasion for her sake and will, as noted earlier, admire you and feel that you are wise and likely to be right for her. Your staying there also makes her feel that you are trustworthy, for why else would you put up with discomfort for her sake? This often results in your succeeding with her but not knowing why, at least at the moment of encounter. Your understanding will catch up with you later and you will soon see what made the connection work out well for you.

The attitude of taking chances for success has a place here because your efforts are likely to feel risky, at least in the beginning. This changes quickly, and happily, as soon as you have the good experience of seeing why you succeeded where you did. When you do not see why things went as they did remind yourself that your continued efforts will bring you the understanding you want, and then relish looking forward to it. As always with females, they will sense that you are doing a difficult thing because you want them and that will help you to succeed, even when you are not sure about what is happening. This is one example of how a success attitude keeps your eyes on your goal and keeps you in motion towards it, rather than letting doubts or other negative emotions slow you.

It is especially worthwhile in your early work at success to commit to taking action for what you want at once, without delay and regardless of what inner feelings may seem to not be with you. When you feel like delaying or postponing turn your attention to the rewards that await you, and give your best first efforts to the charmer whose company you want to enjoy. A success attitude uses the rewards you want to attract you to the measures that work, rather than to avoiding what you do not want. The view of what life will soon bring you will give you an energy that you will enjoy. You will also find that the females you wish for like what it does to them, though you may not see this at first. That energy gives you a lively way that sets you in motion towards them. It also jump starts the discovery principle because your energy tends to make an obvious show of itself, making it easy for a female to see how much you like what you find in her.

Growth in the art of success is like a love relation in some ways. What's male is male because its feminine part is lesser and the obvious parallel holds for females. Nature uses these proportions to make love and romance delectable, for a male's feminine side is awakened by his lover, as a female's masculine side is by her lover. As a man commits to success he becomes more masculine, but the personal growth that creates the success wakes up his feminine part even more. The art of success brings you closer to what a woman wants and nearer to seeing how you already are what she wants, as well as how to offer it to her. These things make you more aware of your make up and hers. Your close up look at such things opens you to the feminine side of being a male, and this is very potent in attracting women.

This power to attract that comes as you grow the art is inevitable for more reasons than the ways you acquire. A woman can only be drawn to a man who speaks her language because that is a basis for a personal connection. This is very similar to finding someone in a foreign place that speaks your mother tongue. In addition, the insight and ways that create success want and need the part of your personality that is more feminine, because that is the part of you that is richer in feeling, intuition and the power to grow. Women love finding this in men, as you will discover for yourself. Put differently, the art of success awakens a part of you that women can only see in themselves and therefore welcome.

Positioning yourself for success puts you into the flow of a process. Much of the success process is learning the simple, but not always easy, lesson that releasing your first feelings for the one you want will almost always win her for you. The more you let yourself flow to your goals with your eyes on what you want, the more your own personality will do the work for you. It is a matter of letting go and letting the way of nature carry you. This means that nature made you to succeed when you want to and nature has also given you the means to succeed. You get to the success you want by going with what she, the female who gets to you, does to you and letting it go out to her. A large part of a success attitude is learning to go with the flow of this emotional process, trusting that nature has made you and her well enough for this to work out happily. As you grow in the art you will see this happening more and more, first with others who do it well and then with yourself. If the personal powers that you need are not evolved enough when you begin, then nature will join your wish and grow them up from within you, as long as you are committed to your success.

Getting into the mood or feeling that you are flowing with the process that goes where you wish to go is a sign of entering the middle phase of the art. You can accelerate your gains at this point by studying women with each other. Most women not only go more easily with the emotional flow of life but also enjoy it so much that they seek it out. To repeat, their way is to know life and the world by how it makes them feel, and this makes them eager to sense where the flow is and to let it carry them. Their way is a thing to be studied and imitated on your journey. As always, a female seeing that your way reminds her of her own way, will find you seductive, feel you are wise and want to be with you. This leads to a very practical measure: when you are unsure of how to ride your feelings to where they want to go, pick a female you know and watch her do it first. Her goal is not likely to be the same as yours, but the process that she gives herself to more easily than men will be the same and therefore be worth your study.

A success attitude looks far more to the process and the goals that the process leads to than to the use of methods or techniques. In fact, you will get the most from the principles with an attitude that keeps your eyes on the process that moves you to your goals and keeps you in its flow. The key role of discipline here, indeed its only role, is to be ready to make the next effort whether or not the last one pleased you. In preparing for a next foray, it is best to draw energy from thoughts and images of what it would be like to beguile the lady who beguiles you, rather than undertaking a forced march.

It is fun and worthwhile to play with the umbrella technique or to power through ambivalence, but going with the flow of emotion and sensation that makes you want to do the things that work is even better. As noted, the wishes that a female's beauty fill you with are given by a nature that also gives you the means to realize them. As you learn to flow with what that lovely lady sets in motion within you, you will feel nature showing you your way to what you want. That way will be, of course, in releasing the free and happy expressions of what she does to you. That way is what you will experience as you position yourself for success by riding the flow of a process attitude.

For some men it is better, at first, to more work on a success attitude than with the principles. A good success attitude creates energy and sustains you while you grow the art. Once you have an understanding of the principles you will soon begin to enjoy more success. How long it takes any one male to improve depends on where he starts from. If the principles are clear to you and you are not satisfied with how quickly success grows, then it is a good idea to ask how energized you are. This question leads to the idea of attitude and how you position yourself for the success you want.

Attitude and the principles are related roughly as fuel to engine. If your engine is in good order but has trouble getting up to speed, then it would be a good idea to check your fuel. If your fuel is sound, but the ride is too slow then it would be wise to check your engine. These two sentences mean that when you know you can do better, then you either know the principles but need more attitude to get further, or you are energized and in flow but need more work with the principles to better place your efforts. These are simple but very powerful ideas for you to apply in growing the ways that form the art of success. As always, the more you grow success with women, the more you grow success in your life overall.

The Appendix after this final chapter gives you answers to success FAQs. The answers give you a feeling for both the principles and the attitude towards them that works best. Put differently, the Appendix will help you to take in both this chapter and the one before it, and to put them together. The principles that form the art of success are a result of many years of research and testing. Positioning yourself for success, or attitude, is a piece of wisdom that has been known for many centuries. For the great majority of men, it works better to first prepare to act by learning what the principles mean and to begin to find their meaning in life around you. Then, when you are about to give yourself to growing the art, take a little time to see how much positive energy and eager anticipation your success attitude gives you. This is one of the points where the FAQs can help you a great deal.

It is easy to see when you are using the success principles correctly because more success will follow immediately upon your doing so. You will be there with the female you set your hopes on to watch the results of what you know you did, and this makes finding your outcome a certainty. When it comes to attitude, there are even more obvious signs of your getting into what works.

Recall for a moment a time when you were exercising and your attention drifted away from what you were doing. At such a time you were lost to what you were doing, probably only to catch up with yourself and realize that your body was doing the exercise and you were elsewhere. This is very similar to what happens when you enter the flow of the process of success. You will find yourself lost to your flirtations and enjoying them. It will come to you in the middle of it all that your personality is doing the work for you and, in a sense, you are watching it happen. Moments like this are a sure sign of getting into the flow.

There is no flow when success does not come because negative outcomes quickly end the pursuit. This means that you will not find yourself watching yourself, and feeling good about it, when you are not moving toward success. In fact, you are not at all likely to lose yourself to what you do when it is less than what you want. Nature made your personality too well for it not to remind you that you need to change what you are doing for things to go better. The deeper part of your personality, that knows very well how to succeed, also knows when to abort and change the approach.

Please feel free to contact me. The Appendix and the final page tell you how to reach me. What comes now can be among the most rewarding and exciting times of your life. What you acquire in the art of succeeding with women will bring you more of the love and romance that you want for the rest of your life. Your personal investment in learning how to succeed will keep returning dividends throughout your life, and the more you invest the greater your return. You have much to look forward to and I give you my best wishes for your success with that amazing other gender. Bon voyage! Bon appetit!

APPENDIX: SUCCESS FAQs

The frequently asked questions (FAQs) given here were gathered at the website Success FAQs on Singles, Dating & Relationships. The FAQs are listed below and the replies to them follow. You can submit new questions or communicate with the author at the website. Its URL is www.successways.com.

FAQ 1: How do women want men to flirt with them?
FAQ 2: What is a good way to handle a woman who gives you mixed messages?
FAQ 3: What do women feel is hard to find in men?
FAQ 4: Why is dancing so important to women?
FAQ 5: What can I do with how anxious flirting makes me?
FAQ 6: Sometimes women can be so silly. Is there a message in this?
FAQ 7: How do I flirt to hold a woman's interest?
FAQ 8: What can I do to keep my last relation from interfering with my next one?
FAQ 9: Is it a good idea to be in touch with a former lover?
FAQ 10: I have seen men who seem irresistible to women. How do they do that?
FAQ 11: How do I deal with the differences between men and women?
FAQ 12: How can I to get to women as much as they get to me?
FAQ 13: Just how does a man make a woman feel?
FAQ 14: Why do women become so angry over bad endings?
FAQ 15: What do women really want from men?

FAQ 16: What are women likely to be up to when they seem too crafty?
FAQ 17: How do I deal with my lover's betrayal?
FAQ 18: What are transitional relations and why are they so risky?
FAQ 19: Why do women seek men who treat them badly?
FAQ 20: How can I approach a woman for a first date when I don't know her?
FAQ 21: Do men have any advantage over women?

FAQ 1: How do women want men to flirt with them?

Women want you to flirt with them because it reassures them of their beauty and value. They feel that what you see in them creates the good things you send them in your flirtation. The more you key into how they see themselves, the more successful you will be.

It pays to flirt with confidence and not just in yourself, but in her too. She wants to see that you see just how worthwhile she is. The more you go to her expecting her to be open to you, the more she will welcome you. It is very important to approach her as a gentleman. She will take your courtesy as a good first sign that you are someone she will want to learn about. Your politeness also tells her that you see how valuable she is as a person.

If she gets to you enough to make you want to try to connect with her, then let your feelings show. She wants to see the good things she can do to you. Women set great value by how much they can create good feelings in men just by your eye finding them.

Flirting is the premier time and place to let your feelings of joy and hope show. The more obvious you make your delight in her and your hopes for her, the more she will feed off of what she is doing to you. Do this with a clear respect for her as a person and she won't want you to go away.

FAQ 2: What is a good way to handle a woman who gives you mixed messages?

Get to work on appealing more strongly to the positive part of her messages. A woman's most basic of all needs with men, to be found desirable for what she is, will study your offer with great interest. The prospect of your genuine interest in her leading to good things between you will take root in her. Your ongoing yen for her will attract her favor and make her other kind of messages pale away.

Women are no more comfortable with ambivalence than men. They often resign themselves to it as part of their biology. When they step into their rich intuitions they are at risk of losing perspective. At such times their thoughts often turn to what it is like to be a man. They know instinctively that men's emotions have a different relation to their decisions and actions. This means that there is a bright prospect in her mixed messages.

She will take in your sustained interest in her with an inner need to make your male energy her own. Your masculine way promises her something she cannot give herself. It is very likely to settle her ambivalence in your favor. At a deeper level within herself she will feel grateful for your helping hand.

FAQ 3: What do women feel is hard to find in men?

To a woman a relationship is a way to fulfillment and personal growth — hers and yours. Men usually find more of color and excitement in it.

Women know how much they can light up a man's life. They give little thought to how much men want the sweet energy they offer. Their concern is more with the stability of the relation. She is very concerned with holding on to what she needs from you. Your male ways put a sense of grounding in her life. This is not something she can give herself enough of alone. She wants to feel secure about you being there. Your lively interest in her brings her a welcome sense of reassurance about you, almost like a hug that keeps on going.

A woman who feels that she can count on the fellow in her life will want to bless him with many rewards. They know instinctively how to please and will give in abundance to the man they feel is trustworthy. She needs to trust that you will find more beauty in her tomorrow than today. And she wants to know you will be there for her with support and tender concern.

FAQ 4: Why is dancing so important to women?

It is easier for a woman to have a rush of good feelings than for a man. Their bodies are more elastic and they revel more easily in their emotional energy. Put differently, it is much easier for a woman to turn on to playful motion than for a man. This is an important part of herself that she wants to share with the fellow in her life. It comes from how immediate a woman's emotions are to her as compared to a man.

Dancing with her is also a statement to everyone present that you find her attractive. She feels that she can judge how much you value and appreciate her by how much you enjoy dancing with her. Your awkwardness, if any, will count for little next to how much you enjoy being near her on the dance floor.

At a deeper level women feel that men who like to dance with them are more emotionally connected to them. She will give you her smile in gratitude for the dance and even more for savoring the color she puts into it. Women find dancing so exciting because your interest in it lights up their inner feelings of glee, and this adds to a more willing spirit and anatomy to start with.

FAQ 5: What can I do with how anxious flirting makes me?

Women love it when you take risks for their sake. She knows that you are risking rejection and other bad feelings when you decide to try your luck with her. That's why it pays to accept your anxiety as part of the flirtation. She will respect you for putting up with the discomfort you accept for her sake.

Women do not care one way or the other if you are anxious. They are interested in how you deal with it. She will see your commitment to flirt with her in spite of your anxiety as an expression of deep strength in you. She will admire your vigor and will be likely to view it as gallant, a most treasured thing in their eyes.

Call upon your sense of humor for help. It goes a long to dissolve your own discomfort. Wit and whimsy are another trait that women find desirable in men. She sees in your eyes how you fancy her. Show her how your sporting ways and glee rise above your anxiety and she will feel compelled to let you into her life.

FAQ 6: Sometimes women can be so silly. Is there a message in this?

Their silliness comes from one of their very best parts. Their feelings leap quickly and easily into what comes their way, much more so than for men. When she is silly with you she is telling you about the rush of good feelings she gets when you are near. Her message is that she wants to share with you how nice the world is with you in it.

Women share their inner feelings of play or joie de vivre with men they trust and whose interest they hope to win. They value their delightful ways highly because they know how much they can light up someone else's life. They give themselves these things all the time and they very much want you to see the magical energy they have in store for you.

Her silliness invites you to play with her. It is an invitation a mile wide to frolic with her because she likes what she sees in you. She is giving you a key to getting closer to her, and fast. She will love you for playing with her and sharing a part of herself that she values greatly. She will take your glee as a sign that you understand her and that you prize her make up.

Women admire a sporting instinct in men. A throw away attitude towards life's risk also throws away her anxieties and draws her interest your way. She sees a welcome relief from her inner concerns when you play with her.

Women usually assume that men are unwilling to freely express themselves. They will feel that you are in good touch with yourself when you play with them. And they will take your play as coming from your perception of the good things in them. Your play, or teasing, works to lift the anxiety of the moment and opens up to you the rewards she has in mind to give you.

FAQ 7: How do I flirt to hold a woman's interest?

Many things are in your favor from the outset. She assumes that you are at an advantage because you are a man. Her view is that if you don't favor her then you will simply move on and find someone else. She wants your strength and affection in her life. The key to your advantage is in knowing what kind of a delivery she is hoping you will give her.

Market your ways with a sporting attitude. Some lightheartedness will make both of you more comfortable. She will respect how you manage the challenge and you will win her first interest. Give her large doses of your sweet interest. Women have a very deep wish for men who are fascinated by their personalities. Relate to her as if there is no other female anywhere and she will be hypnotized by your interest. She will also think you are very wise and perceptive.

Women assume that you find them sexually attractive. They want to know how they make you feel. They take your joy in their personal makeup as a sign of healthy interest in them. They will invite you in for more when they feel that you are really interested in what their emotional makeup can do to you.

Women see sex more as a reward for your good interest in them than as something they want for themselves. And she will move heaven and earth for the man whom she knows to be interested enough in her as a person.

FAQ 8: What can I do to keep my last relation from interfering my next one?

Take a break to deal with your feeling of hurt or anger. Wait for the negative feelings to give way to a leisurely openness to someone new. Your next relation can prosper by what you can learn about yourself in the time after your last one.

The next woman in your life will want to see the finer side of you. Go to work on releasing your last relation to the past. Recall what was good and satisfying about it. Treat the dark side of it as something that you are parting with and look upon it without blaming yourself or her.

The next woman will sense your feelings toward your last lover. She will be glad to see that you cherish what was good about it and she will admire you for releasing your negative feelings. Your next lover will become anxious that she is not getting enough of you if she feels that you are still in the midst of strong negative feelings from the past. When she sees that the majority of your energy is going toward her, she will be eager to draw you on with her sweetness and emotional richness.

FAQ 9: Is it a good idea to be in touch with a former lover?

This can bring you gains in personal growth if you want to be in touch for a higher purpose. Letting her know that you savor the better part of what you had and that you do not fault yourself or her for where it did not work is an example. Her good feelings for how you work the end of your relation are sure to make for better in your next one.

It is also a good idea to be in touch if it helps you to move on. Sometimes a last round of contact is necessary to release the ties that hold you up. It could be time to return for a look/see with the larger you that grew after it ended. An open and caring tryst with her can return you to life with a great deal of liberating insight into her, you and what happened between you. And likewise for her.

It may also bring a welcome relief to your former lover to learn that you are moving on towards more good things in life. A healthy woman will want this for you as you will want it for her. The next female in your life will love you more for finding better in her and for not stewing with resentment over your last one. She will see your attitude as decent, a trait that women are quick to admire and want more of.

FAQ 10: I have seen men who seem irresistible to women. How do they do that?

There are two kinds of men who seem to do far better with women than most others. Actors, athletes and others familiar as media stars are one kind. They offer glamorous attraction to lofty and dreamed of parts of life that others have little or no access to. They can satisfy a woman's need for reverie and romance. This has very little to do with women want from men as men.

The playing field levels when it comes to what women want in a relation. The really irresistible fellow has certain personality traits that invite women on for more. A man who is in touch with his own make up unwittingly tells a woman that he can be in touch with hers. This is a very exciting idea to a woman because the majority of what she wants is your eyes on her experience of herself.

A splash of charm helps. Think of charm as a higher form of authenticity or self acceptance. Charm goes out with the expression of certain colorful parts of yourself. This is a natural thing for a man who lives at ease with his emotions. There is no need to study charm because it comes by itself as you let more of yourself in.

So what about that seductive guy who gets all the gals? If he wants a relation or anything else from a woman that lasts longer than a brief encounter then he is on the level part of the playing field. Sexual magnetism is a wonderful seasoning for what women want first and foremost: your interest in them and how they are made.

FAQ 11: How do I deal with the difference between men and women?

Noting that the sexes are much more alike than different is a good beginning. Most of your experience as a male agrees with hers as a female. This means that you can already read or anticipate most of her wishes, hopes and concerns.

Men have everything that women have and vice versa. The difference is in the degree to which each gender has it. The gender difference is small, not large.

The idea is to know where it is real and where it is important.

Women are more emotional than men. Even the size of the brain region that does emotional processing is larger in women than in men. Men are usually more directed and focused than women. This difference draws a line in the sand when it comes to meeting and connecting.

On her side of the line she sends her meanings out more in her feelings than in what she does or even says. And she expects you to get her meaning the way she does: with your feelings. On your side your meanings go out in words and actions. And you expect her to find your meaning in what you say and do.

If men's emotional makeup were as immediate as women's then they would get a woman's message every time. And if women were as centered and directed as men then they would get a man's meaning every time.

A good way to deal with the major difference between men and women is to see that your own emotional make up is amplified in her. Likewise, your own action makeup has a back seat to the high volume of her emotional makeup. The more you look for how what you do and say makes her feel, the better you will fare with her.

A woman knows and judges her life and world very much by the way it stirs her emotions. Men make the judgment more with logical thinking and a wish to take action in the world. A woman may admire this in you but she will not understand it the same way as you. She will first look for the effect of what you do on how she feels.

FAQ 12: How can I to get to women as much as they get to me?

Women want to be slow and coy about how seductive they find you because they first want assurances elsewhere. It is harder for a woman to manage her growing feelings of interest and excitement over a man than vice versa. She will give her best efforts to staying in charge of how much you reach her in order to keep her attention on the other parts of you.

Women go chemical over your male ways. Your strength of purpose and steadfast ways get to them from the very first. And let it be said that they want your physical strength and sense of mastery in their lives because it turns them on. These things go out from you as free samples of a kind. Make them work for the rest!

Your self esteem and regard for yourself as a person of value will increase your value in her eyes. Let her see your desire for her and her sexual charms as part of a larger bargain. It is important for her to know that your wish for her will not let you compromise your own worth. She will respect and understand this because women are prouder creatures than men when it comes to their desirability.

You can get to her in a big way and quickly by challenging her, non-verbally of course, to meet and match your worth. You can do this by sending her your desire for her with the added message that you will not give the store away. Giving her what she does to you with what you might do to her can bring her interest beyond what her coy and measured ways can deal with.

Women usually feel that their sexual offerings alone are enough to win a man's interest and favor. There is great leverage in her seeing that this is not true of you. Let her know how you prize yourself and that you want more. She will accept this and work to get you in her life.

FAQ 13: Just how does a man make a woman feel?

When a woman sees a look of favor in your eyes she leaps with excitement to you. She hopes to experience an energy that men have much more of than women. Her excitement over your interest in her takes a back seat to her desire to see your ways pour into her. Women long for more of what they usually call male purpose or focus.

They cannot help admiring how much stronger men are than women. This is one basis for their wishing to have your support in their lives. Their hope for your dynamism can simply undo them when you hold them close. You can measure how much they see strength of purpose and togetherness in you by how much they lose it when you draw near to them.

Men who are empathic or a little sensitive are at an advantage with women. Women are more than eager to take such personal traits as being similar to their own. A woman sees a man in touch with or sensitive to his feelings as very well prepared to share her experience of herself, and to benefit by it.

Give your male ways to a woman with polite interest and kindness and she will be likely to lose her composure. And she will lose it in your favor. That's how you make them feel.

FAQ 14: Why do women become so angry over bad endings?

Women see themselves more as the creators of a relation than men do. In their eyes they give a special feeling and energy that makes the relation possible in the first place. They know that nature has made them feel fit to give all that they are to one person. Her emotions are richer and stronger than a man's and she wants to give them generously to you and the relation.

It is important to a woman that the fellow she gives herself to sees and appreciates these things. Her desirability is at issue. Large offers want large recognitions. That is why it is so important to a woman to feel discovered by the man she cares for. She knows how much she has in mind to give him and she wants him to see its value. She wants him to savor the good things he can get from her and not by himself alone.

The worst of the bad endings for a woman is in feeling that she has misinvested herself. Her large offerings draw upon so much of her that a poor ending leaves her feeling empty and cheated by fate. Her anger will follow the man who too little appreciated her offerings or who took them for granted.

Women measure their own worth by how well the relationship works. They see themselves as inviting you to it and they see you as its beneficiary. Their sense of dignity prospers as you and the relation prosper. The relation that fails, in her eyes, because her fellow did not welcome the gift of herself comes to her as a blow to her dignity. Women do not fare as well as men when it comes to issues of dignity.

At bottom a woman wants a man to work with her purpose. Her trust is centered on feeling that he wants to feed off of her ways and that he will give the relation a firm center. Women feel betrayed when trust fails or when they find that the meaning of the relation is undone. Such events open a deep sense of loss and indignity in them. There is no parallel in men to the storm of anger that follows their hurt.

There is some temptation to feel that the insincere man purchases such an outcome. It is not so simple. A man who honestly feels she is not right for him, when she feels that she is, will receive the same fury as the gigolo. Nothing is more important to a woman who has eyes for you than that you find her worthy.

FAQ 15: What do women really want from men?

Almost every woman wants you to see her as beautiful. She sees her beauty as just beginning in the way she looks and is formed. She feels that the larger part of her beauty is in her emotional makeup and personality. A woman sees herself more in psychic terms than a man. They want your eyes to enjoy how they look and they want much more that your eyes will move on to the larger attractions they feel within.

A women bases her trust in you on how much and how well your attention moves from how she looks to what she is like as a person. She sees her inner world as the most beautiful and enduring thing about herself. The man who has a sense for her emotional life will win much favor in her eyes and quickly. She sees her greatest gift to you in the way her person can enrich and uplift your life. A woman wants love making to enter after she is confident that you have some sense of what it means to her feelings.

Her wish for you to be one with her inner life remains the most important thing to her. In her eyes, sex and love making are a wonderful expression of the trust she has in you. In fact, she will go on seeing your love making as her gift to you for being a trustworthy person who is in touch with her.

Women know what their emotional energy can do to men. They know what it means to be the main event in a man's life. That is why it is so important to them that you appreciate how they experience themselves. The more you connect with what you do to her feelings, the more she will light up your life with her winning ways.

There are things in men that women wish they could possess. They need more than just your appreciation of what they are like and how they look. They wish to have a man's sense of strong purpose and focus in their lives. They need this because their emotions can easily take off and make them feel off center or without balance. They long for how your support makes them feel more together.

Women want to fill your life with themselves and their color. And they want to have your masculine way firmly in their lives. The power of your male way gives her a feeling of completeness that she cannot have by herself alone.

FAQ 16: What are women likely to be up to when they seem too crafty?

Her emotional shrewdness or craft is most likely to be an effort to control the way you come together. She may be overawed by you and have a need to slow things down for a while. This is a bright prospect best welcomed by your easing up on her. Signs of tension, awkwardness or anxiety in her would be telltale in this case.

It may be that she is genuinely fearful of getting close to a man. Her similar behavior around other men will give this away. Your patience and support will mean a great deal to her if she has this kind of apprehension. If you want to pursue her then you should eventually talk to her about it. This kind of problem is solvable when she wants it to be and is otherwise likely to bring you little more than frustration and lost hope.

A woman may express the immature side of herself with sly or even aggressive ways. This is a common way of dealing with inner feelings of weakness or insufficiency. The charm in her girlish abandon to what she is doing tells you that a less evolved part of her is talking to you. If she charms you overall then accept this part of her too, as you would want her to do if the shoe were on the other foot.

FAQ 17: How do I deal with my lover's betrayal?

This is an area where a man's first way can work against him. Both genders have the same healthy answer to betrayal. The better reply comes more easily to women. The lovely other gender is rarely surprised to learn that their lover's heart belongs to another woman. The subtle ways that make men long for them are better suited to mending a heart broken by betrayal than the male's directness.

Anger lives in the wake of hurt or pain. Confusion and vengeful images follow the discovery that her heart really belongs to someone else. The search for an action to fit the event spends energy in vain. A man's first reply to a problem in life is usually to gear up for action. This reply answers well to the outer world. A wound like betrayal asks a man to take leave of the outer world for a while. Seeking new parts of the inner self to recreate life after this kind of event comes more easily to a woman's nature.

A wounded female is unlikely to again ask why it happened once she accepts that she has been betrayed. Her way is quick to see that the problem begun in the outer world wants to be solved from within. She loses little time engaging the feelings of hurt and injury where they live. She gives herself to living the pain and leaving the anger for as long as it takes for the hurt to sire a new and better self. The shortest route from the pain to renewal gives patient acceptance to betrayal's aftermath. The female psyche that promises men poetic joy also knows more about healing itself.

It is wise to watch and not become a part of inner dialogues as you become one with the hurt. There is temptation to obsess over why it happened, how you might have averted it and such. This sends energy to the wrong place. Obsessing is like trying to avoid a whirlpool by heading for its center. The first part of the remedy is to feel more and to think or speculate less.

The inner chatter will always be there. Health wants you to stand above it and not be one with it.

Appendix: Success FAQs 315

Send your attention to your wound and let the rush of thoughts blow their own wind. The feminine way lives as a second to a man's first way just as the masculine way is second to a woman's. Mourning your loss and arising from it wants your second way to take center stage.

In time your emotions will clear. Mark your speed by how quickly you choose to own them. A better view of what happened will grow from the heart and replace heady speculations. A newly forming you heals the wound by feeding on the storm's power. Higher wisdom and fresh energy await you as growth patiently fuels itself on the storm.

Chances are that she gave herself to the relation in good faith and that circumstance decided its fate. The likely finding that the current of life drove her elsewhere silences ideas of malice on her part. Accepting that life itself could have pulled you away opens you to compassion and invites you to higher ground. She probably had no more ability to alter what life sent her than what it sent you.

Easy gain and faster healing live where the exception is true. Learning that she acted with malice undoes the attachment to her by itself. It finds a lie in what gave itself as true worth and sends your interest elsewhere. Her deception will quickly return you to life for the joy of better intended women. The wound came from what you thought she was and vanishes in learning otherwise.

Closure tells you to release her to where she chose to go. Sending her back to her own life will lift your self esteem. You have the power to release her and she does not. Betrayal happened because it happened and that's the sum of it. It could easily have happened the other way and then the likely innocence of it all would be easier to see.

Use the way of all women to end the hurt of one woman. Every love relation wants each gender to become more like the other. Go to your lesser, feminine side where the other way lives. It will speed your healing and return you to life in a larger way.

FAQ 18: What are transitional relations and why are they so risky?

A mate brings many wonderful goods to your life. The high regard for the other as someone special lifts your esteem. Your lover's trustworthy presence makes your life feel more grounded and worthwhile. Your mate gives you energy, makes you feel happy to be alive and sends you into life with a flourish. And it is likewise for the other.

When a long term relationship ends so does the supply of these emotional blessings. It does not matter if one, the other or both chose to end the relation. The instant effect is a loss of self esteem and a need find support elsewhere. That once significant other who made her feel so special and life so right is no longer there. The need to again feel special and to have a secure grounding becomes a hunger. Self esteem, whose sweet energy makes life happy and successful, is threatened with sudden decline.

The need to feel special and worthwhile assumes a life of its own and soon commands her first attention. Recently divorced people and others ending long term relations are eager to rush into a next relation. There is a wonderfully charming energy in their ways. Their openness to the next person is so seductive, so energized that it seems no answer but "Yes" is possible to them.

The person who takes her offer is the transitional relationship and has chosen to walk on emotional thin ice. The new charmer in your life is driven to find her worth in your adulation over her. And how do you not believe that her eager energy will not go on and on and on? Well, you shouldn't because it will end and with the speed of a torch put into water when it does.

The transitional need to be propped up by a new lover lasts about two years on average. In this period she is working through the loss of her former mate or lover and is finding emotional fuel in your welcome. This is a normal, natural and healthy behavior following the end of a long term and deep relation with someone. It is not a form of exploitation and is just as true for men as it is for women.

When she has worked through her loss she will suddenly lose interest in you. You will hear of a yen for space and discovery. Her real message to you is that she can now be self propelled. She needs to send herself back to life on her own and to get a fresh perspective on who and what she is and wants from life.

It is unlikely that she will return to you after she leaves in search of her new and larger self. She will keep her gratitude to you for being there when she needed you. In fact, she will put it among her most cherished memories. There may even be prospects of a friendship. The transitional flame burns very brightly but it only burns once. It leaves a survivor and a victim behind.

There are times when it is wise to accept a woman in search of a transitional relation. If you also are coming out of a long term and close relation then you will both have the same kind of "destined to burn out need." The prospects in this case are rosy. Both will be survivors and neither a victim, regardless of who is first to say farewell.

There are exceptions. Don't let the true story to follow lead you to accept a transitional relation coming your way, unless you are fond of trouble. A friend of mine was divorced for several years and ready for a next relation in the healthiest sense of the word. He met someone and did he ever fall in love! She was finalizing her divorce when they met. He had a grand time with her sparkling energy and wide open welcome for about eighteen months.

Then the bottom fell out. She said she wanted space. She said he was crowding her and limiting her life. She said many things to send him away. He was in a sorry state and clung to hope that she would find a way back to him. I told him that such an outcome was very unlikely. I added that if she did return it would be after a period of self discovery and that his presence in her life at this time would only slow her up.

He tucked his tail between his legs and waited. They met a couple of times a month for coffee and conversation. My friend loved her enough to let her go and knew that his hopes were slim. The story has a Hollywood ending. After about a year of dating other men and learning more about herself she wanted him back. She found that he was right for her after all. This became clear after she worked through the end of her marriage and found the parts of herself that her marriage kept her from. My friend made a strong appeal to the part of her that her first marriage left unfulfilled.

I was happy that my friend beat the odds. The moral of the story is to avoid a transitional relation if you are looking for a relation that will go somewhere other than hurt. This kind of relation can find a good place in your life if you are in the same boat or if you are just looking to have fun with no eye for commitment. In the latter case you risk falling under her spell and will then be at high risk of sudden loss.

FAQ 19: Why do women seek men who treat them badly?

Adolescent and young women, say under 25, often have this preference. What's more, they usually have a need for it. They see power and risk taking behavior as reassuring signs of strength. And for as much as they savor it, they eventually outgrow it.

The real issue is where they are psychologically. Females between puberty and early adult life are anxious within about leaving home and finding their way in life. Males of the same age have less of such concern than females. A young male's bravado and abandon over dangerous pastimes can go a long way to quell her inner fears. Deep within she knows the time is drawing near for her to make a go of life on her own. The real and scary risks are well known to her unconscious but have little access to her waking mind — yet.

A blustery male can dupe a young woman into believing in his invulnerability. And he may also believe his own myth. These things, like the root fear of leaving home, are little known to her conscious mind. Her conscious experience is one of thrill and excitement with his triumph in reckless and dangerous situations. It is breathtaking proof that with him she is safe and out harm's way.

In time she will realize that it was all a beguiling ruse of nature trying to give her the pluck to leave the secure nest of home. At this later time women look back and laugh, usually with an inner sense of what it all meant. This is why one often hears mature women sharing laughter with comic tales of the young men they once found so seductive.

The preference for rough males should end somewhere in the mid- twenties. The young woman's longing for a warrior matures into a high regard for a man's sense of purpose and his power to stay focused. It turns itself into a special fondness for men who are responsible.

A woman who chronically wants rough treatment in her love life has a problem. What is normal, even healthy, for a teenager or young adult is unhealthy for a woman past say her mid-twenties. Seeking shabby treatment or pain serves a purpose in a masochist. Its unhealthy goal is usually to relieve unconscious guilt.

This works something like the process of confession. Some relief of guilt follows the humiliation of confessing to a crime. Conscious pain offers a masochist some relief of guilt unknown to the waking mind. Masochists know that what hurts them also delights them yet they rarely understand why this is so. They tend to attract males who have the flip side of their own problem, the sadists.

There is a place for some of the rougher side at all ages. The thrill of danger is real, exciting and often healthy. People of all ages take to mountain climbing, skiing, sky diving and other sports that involve personal risk. The key idea in matters of the heart is how much thrill over danger the relationship wants.

Your own good judgment will decide if she wants too much of the wild side in a relation. Chances are that if her preferences make you anxious then you would be wise to move on to someone who wants more of your tenderness and less of your power.

FAQ 20: How can I approach a woman for a first date when I don't know her?

You can make a successful first connection with a woman almost every time by letting her see the good feelings and hopes that she inspires in you. Seeing what they do to men is the single most basic need in females after adolescence. It is a need that grows stronger as they mature. It is also important that she feels your approach fits the situation where you find each other. Otherwise she may feel her dignity is at risk or that you have poor judgment.

It can be enough to give a female who draws you on a shy smile when it is likely that you will see her again. This tells her in a courteous way that you already have a happy sense of what she can add to your life. The shy smile moves with her own ways for shyness has the patience that a woman gives to the feelings that your image awakens in her. A female needs time for her new emotions to reach enough parts of herself to take their measure. This is one reason why women almost always have more patience than men.

She will also take your demure advance as announcing your wish to pursue her. Your first lively interest in her will make her hope that you will approach her with the easy tempo of a gentleman. Your polite advance tells her of your esteem for her. It also tells her that you are so taken with her ways that you will study how she reveals the courteous approach she so much wants.

Women have a deeper need than men to let the feelings you sire in them run their full course. A man becomes filled with rushes of good feelings upon seeing a woman he favors. Their very next thoughts are on the practical issue of how to connect. Women have those first rushes also. They find them delicious and want to savor their full run. They know that this may take one or more days and that this seems to work against how quickly most men would like to arrive at their goal. She needs to live with all the good feelings you bring her till she knows their meaning well enough. She does this with relish and as she nears its end she hopes more and more for your next appearance.

When you next see her she is likely to feel ready to go a step nearer to you and what you want. She will want to see your desire in your eyes. She will also be more open to you, wanting to learn more about what it is you see in her that so strikes your fancy and pulls you to her. This will be obvious in the way she gives you time and opportunity to do more than just smile at her the next time you meet. That next encounter is a good time to tell her what she already knows, that the mere sight of her makes you feel good all over and that you hope for more. This is a natural time to tell her your name and ask for hers.

If you let what she does to you show then she will linger before you waiting for more of the same, for you are giving her exactly what her female make up wants from a male. The rest now follows much on its own by staying the course. Your courteous delight in flirting with her and letting your feelings show and tell will all but lead to her asking you out. I recommend that you do the asking once she can no longer cloak her appetite for seeing you revel in her.

Take measures to manage her concern over feeling compromised if this is a one time only opportunity. Send her your playfulness to melt her concerns. Women like to frolic more than men but most men have yet to learn this. Their relish for play is a close cousin to those wonderful feelings that men so much want from them. When you play with a woman she is likely to feel that you understand her as well as desire her. Flirting in a sporting way will put her past her concerns and into wanting to enjoy the sight of how she gets to you.

You can make her smile with a silly but obvious ploy that wins her attention and sends her concerns about propriety to oblivion. The more openly you do this, and with glee, the more likely you are to succeed. The playful risk taking you undertake to win her attention will instantly win her admiration. The last sentence is so important that I hope you will read it again. It is now a short step to winning her wish for you, and the more so if others are present and enjoying your open flirtation. The larger the merry risk you take for her sake, and before others, the more certain you are to win her favor.

It should happen of itself that your expression wears mirth and merriment. This tells her of the good feelings you bring to her, a thing that she will take to be her creation in you. There is little need for you to be creative for she wants to see the good feelings that the sight of her gives you. This is why pre-rehearsed lines work against you: she wants to see what she does to you then and there, not something you thought about and felt long before. She wants to know she has reached you and she wants to see it in the natural way you give back to her, in your expressions, what she does to you. Do this with a lighthearted acceptance of risk for her sake and you are as certain to succeed as you can be.

She is likely to be smiling before you say a word if you have let loose in your expressions the prospects you see in her and your intent for some fun and laughter. It matters little what you now say. It can be almost anything such as "You make a great first impression. I want to do the same with you" or "Your ways are just too nice to ignore." She will take your offerings with relish and wait for more because you are giving her what all women want: to have a man so taken with the discovery of their beauty and promise that he takes open risks for their sake.

Do this from a position of self esteem and with some giggles and you are likely to put all her concerns on having more of you. Women rarely find men who understand their need to be discovered by a male who feels his own worth and who is willing to offer himself openly before others for her sake. When they find this highly treasured and innermost dream come to life before them, then all else leaves them but the one remaining wish to watch the dream come true.

The power of your confident wish for her will charm her past her composure. In time she will regain her composure and you will easily see its return. A polite, or better a gracious, request for a way to find her again will enter well into your first encounter with her. You can offer your name and request hers. She is sure to give it without any hesitation at all. It is best to not ask for her telephone number. Her confidence in your regard for her will grow if you ask where you are likely to find her again. You can even arrange then and there to meet in a public place she favors.

There are sound reasons for so much ado about what is proper with women at a first meeting. Women assume you are interested in them from the outset. They know that once they care they will give all to make you happy and make the relationship prosper. As their love grows they release more and more of themselves to you and become possessed by their emotions. It is even fair to say that their emotions live their lives when in love. They feel they may risk giving their hearts away in vain and then learn that they judged poorly. Such concerns are why, in the male's eyes, women make first meetings so difficult. Women see it very differently.

Your smile, your laughter, your obvious joy over being there with her, your approach with high self regard are all parts of a deep inner wish common to all women. When rightly appealed to, women become undone and will offer no answer but yes.

These things were well know to Casanova (1725-1798) whose genius reached far and wide from the arts and sciences to human nature and more. His inner awareness of women's deep wish to be adored for what they are and with honor won the hearts of 132 women. Casanova left only two of these women with less than rosy after memories. Most of his former lovers stayed in close contact with him, so delicious was the taste he left in their mouths. When his fortunes declined in later life many of them returned the expensive gifts he had once given them to help him.

His feelings were real and his intentions of the kindly nature that women simply adore in men. He rushed to be present at the last moments of his first love Bettina, who literally died in his arms (1777). It was Bettina who at age 15 first awakened Casanova to love at age 11. So precise was Casanova's intuition and so real his adoration of women that at least once he cast a spell over a woman in less than a day that happily impelled her to leave her homeland and travel elsewhere with him. All this, for having an exact sense of what the female heart wants and that again, is to regale their wondrous beauty from a position of honor and self worth.

FAQ 21: Do men have any advantage over women?

Most men are remarkably unaware of how and how much they get to women. The sight of him makes her pulse quicken, her breath abandon her and puts her chemistry on tilt. His ways trigger fireworks of emotion in her that she finds delicious and wished for long before he came into view. She finds what he does to her difficult to cloak although she very much wants to keep it from his eyes. An informed man will see through her cool appearance to her struggle to not let him see how much he has gotten to her.

Nature has many joys in mind for the coming together of men and women. The advantage on both sides comes from nature's wish for each to find a larger version of his or her lesser part in the other. What one has less of the other has in greater measure. This is not easy for most males to see. Men usually see large and unfair advantages in women's immense powers of attraction. Their exquisite lines, the rapture in how they move and their magical ways so flood men with desire that men often feel nature gave all the leverage to women. The female powers that send men into altered states of wonder over how to win her are also the key to men's advantage over them.

She is more a creature of feeling than he is and that is one reason she charms him so. He is more a creature of action and purpose than she is and that is one reason he charms her so. She finds some lure in the raw power of a male's frame and greater muscle bulk. A man's greatest power to compel her is in how he can commit himself to action and hold to his purpose. Very few men know how thrilling it is for a woman to see men enter this state of committed action. The near presence, say within a few yards, of a man centered on what is important to him can easily undo a woman and plant her where she stands to look upon him with admiration and desire. Women once expressed this among themselves by calling a man dashing.

She knows more about her advantage than men do. That is why she knows that her edge with men is her also her vulnerability. This is a mystery to most men and it is no mystery at all to women. Their wonderful emotional color and the richness of their ways is a miracle of nature. Women enjoy how easily their feelings sweep over and through them. They know life and the world by the movements of their feelings more than by their gifts of mind and reason. Men rarely come to realize that these movements too often take place too soon, too much and too frequently. Women often feel without center, unfocused and without balance because their emotions become too intense, too dispersed and too unrelated. Enter the man in her life, please.

A woman's advantage comes from giving men emotions they are little able to give themselves. Women are very aware of this and most will admit that they feel it is an unfair advantage on their side. This makes many of them grateful that most men do not realize the male advantage. An admiring female sees a man's power to put distance between his committed purpose and his feelings. He simply will not allow his emotions to interfere with what he intends to finish, whether a thought or an action. This is difficult for women to do. Women envy how much a man can feel centered without anyone's help. That is one reason why women rarely to go social events alone. They need each other's support to give them the centered feeling and focus that comes much more easily to men.

When she first meets him she is watching how well his ways make her feel more grounded and how well he makes her feelings come together. It is a delight for her to feel that she is on top of her feelings instead of in the middle of them or carried along by them. From the eighteenth to the early twentieth century it was fashionable for women to reveal this by swooning. They still swoon inside when they catch sight of a man's firmer way and his power to stand above his emotions in favor of a purpose he will see through. Today one female would tell another of the rush she felt when his energy swept near her rather than of swooning. It means that her many and rich emotions are all going to the same place at the same time: his image. Some women are so undone by this rush of their emotions to one place that they pass out or swoon.

When she is in his arms he is full of joy for the wonder that passes from her to him. There are also major and joyful movements that she welcomes from him to her. The more tenderly he embraces her the more she feels his power over himself enter her and give her a like rising over and above herself. Her emotions are her magic and nature usually overdoes the gift. She needs the male way and cannot give it to herself alone anymore than a male can give himself more emotional richness without a female. In his presence and especially in his arms she feels her lesser power come to fuller life. She is grateful to him for this and rewards him with herself. Men know the reward easily enough and are generally little if at all aware of what they are giving the woman they care for.

What men do to women is a neglected study and women tell little on it. There are telltale signs that give away their treasured secret that you are making them lose their composure. When she sees your male way and how it stands over your emotions she will admire you. Her look is not easy to hide and she wishes it were. When you offer her your interest while taming your anxious concern over how she receives you, her admiration comes in on high tide. If you amble near her you will see her gaze seeking you out when she thinks you are not looking. When you get to her in a large way a tension will form in her neck, for she is trying to keep her gaze away from you or to be ready to quickly remove it if caught in the act. Most women are too proud of their seductive powers to openly announce their desire for you. To tip their hand works against the deepest wish of their nature — to be discovered by an adoring male.

Flirting is a matter of being a braveheart for most men. Every chance taken to win the gift of her beauty runs the risk of failure and unpleasant after feelings. The power that enables a man to put his anxious feelings under control and to venture forward for her sake is a clear expression of what women want more of in themselves. It pays for men to watch how women react to their (dignified) advances. Few men do so. The usual foray has a man's attention on his goal with little, if any, on what he is doing to her. The more a male learns to see that his presence thrills her when she feels the offer of his way to her, the more he will realize that nature has given him an advantage too. It is a large advantage, about equal in power to the explosive hopes that women ignite in men.

The equal advantage between the genders has a divide in it. Women know what they do to men and how they do it. Few men know what they do to women or how. A man who studies this divide and crosses it with insight achieves an advantage so large that the success it brings could easily be seen as unfair. Women's nature tells them all about their advantage and how to work it. They also know that most men do not understand it. Most men need to work at seeing how and how much they replace a woman's composure with the same kind of runaway desires that women fill men with. The shoe is on the other foot. It just takes more work for men to size it.

Dear Reader:

Thank you for reading HOW TO SUCCEED WITH WOMEN. Your input or questions about this book are welcome. You can reach the author by e-mail at afjb@ix.netcom.com or by postal mail at:

>Scientific Support
>19 Crest Street
>Westwood, NJ 07675.

You can order additional copies of HOW TO SUCCEED WITH WOMEN by sending $20.00, check or money order, to Scientific Support at the above address or by calling 201-358-8754.

Best wishes to you!

ABOUT THE AUTHOR

Anthony F. Badalamenti is a research scientist in psychiatry and a psychoanalyst with a private practice. His work on singles' success began in the 1970's and continues. The research behind this book took place in parallel with running singles' groups and research into the dialogue of psychotherapy and of couples.

The author has published more than 50 papers in refereed journals and, together with Robert J. Langs, MD, he published joint research findings on psychotherapy as an exact science in The Cosmic Circle. His work was honored by The Society for Psychoanalytic Psychotherapy in 1990 and has been applied by major research centers.